More Wealth, Less Taxes

ENDORSEMENTS

I wish I'd had this book five years ago when I started on my wealth journey. I've always felt a large burden of needing to be a good steward of my finances, but not knowing if I'm doing the right things with the right advisors. This book has given me peace of mind and helped me course correct my current strategy. It was very helpful to see several real-life case studies and I love that Lance views wealth not just from a financial perspective, but also from a family perspective.

-Eric J. Hinson, CEO of Explainify
and COO of Parable

More Wealth, Less Taxes is an eye-opening must-read for anyone who works, pays taxes, and may someday want to retire. The straightforward analogies, examples, and lessons made it such a fun, easy read. There were so many aha moments as all the investment strategies Lance has been informing us about and doing for us for years clicked. One of the best gifts we can give our children is for them to read this book now so they can have a head start even compared to when we started filling our buckets!

-Gary and Melanie Alecusan, Team Direct
Management, LLC

Lance's practical, straightforward approach helps take the mystery out of preparing for retirement. People at all stages of their journey could benefit from the insights and stories he shares.

-David Karr, Chairman,
Equitable Advisors

Lance has a unique ability to simplify complex ideas, extract the items of highest importance, and present them in a way that is easy to understand. The bucket strategy is ground-breaking. I have already shared this with my family and taken the lessons learned to further lower my own tax bracket. I highly recommend this book to anyone looking to lock in a high level of confidence in their financial future.

-**Mike Prince**, Walmart Vice President, Supply Chain Innovation and Automation

Lance has written a must-read for all those wannabe investors. Speaking for myself as a wannabe, I thought I knew enough to effectively invest. How wrong I was … this book gives great guidance to building long-term wealth while paying fewer taxes in your later years. Aside from his outstanding direction, Lance has always been consistent in his counsel.

-**Blair Etz**, Director of Sales, Shearer's Foods LLC

This book packs a punch for anyone looking to take care of their financial future. The amount of life-changing content is next level.

-**Michael Lieberman**, Partner, Advisors Capital Management

If you want to preserve wealth, decrease your taxes and retire early, this book is for you. I have known Lance for 25 years. Lance was my financial planner in Bentonville, Ark., in 2005. I moved to Dallas a few years later and I tried hard to find a financial planner there because, as they say, everything is "bigger and better in Texas." However, as I searched diligently, it became more apparent that Lance was the best person for the job. He has summarized all his principles into this delightful book, comparing us all to swimmers in the pool of life. His bucket strategy works like a charm, as I have seen him make it work for my family. This thought-provoking book will be useful for most of us to preserve wealth and retire early.

-**Sanjeeb Shrestha**, MD, FACG

I have been a small business owner for 43 years. Without question, tax liabilities have been my greatest struggle. Learning new strategies would have allowed me to keep more of my income in order to make better decisions. I made so many mistakes along the way and now it's too late to recover all that I've lost. Lance takes you on a journey in *More Wealth, Less Taxes* that will keep you from repeating my mistakes.

-**Aaron Walker**, Founder, Iron Sharpens Iron Mastermind

In his new book, Lance Belline condenses his financial planning approach, which took over 25 years to refine, into a step-by-step guide to saving for retirement. This book is a manual that uses real-life examples on how to grow wealth and produce retirement income by limiting potential tax liabilities along the way. Whether you are nearing retirement or beginning your financial journey, Lance's approach to wealth creation and tax savings will help you to gain confidence in your investment decisions and give you clarity in your financial future. *More Wealth, Less Taxes* does a great job of taking high-level financial planning strategies and turning them into a practical guide to help define and achieve your financial goals.

-Luke Brownd, Vice President,
ETFs, First Trust Portfolios

Lance has the experience and a unique gift for bringing transformational clarity and wisdom to building wealth in a tax-efficient way. *More Wealth, Less Taxes* provides a blueprint and great insight into what can be accomplished by being intentional and strategic with your finances. This book is a must-read for those that want to steward their resources well and leave a lasting legacy.

-Blake Brewer, Founder,
Legacy Letter Challenge

Well worth the time to read! An understandable guide to planning—digestible and actionable. Lance covers a ton of ground, from the powerful basics of tax minimization—love the three buckets—to more advanced solutions for business owners, and estate planning. Your tax return and your retirement outlook will improve when you execute on the fundamentals presented here. This is not a textbook, but rather a playbook.

-Jim Mellin, Chief Sales Officer,
Equitable Advisors

I have been working with Lance as a client for 12 years. When he introduced the bucket strategy for retirement savings, I trusted his direction. Now I have peace of mind knowing that my taxable income in retirement will be low, putting more money in my pocket during the golden years. This book gives insights and examples that are helpful and understandable. I highly recommend this book and the bucket strategy!

-**Susan Averitt**, MD

Much of today's financial education focuses mainly on accumulation. In *More Wealth, Less Taxes*, Lance focuses not only on accumulation, but tax-efficient distributions planned in advance. The Bucket Strategy teaches building wealth in a manner that allows keeping, spending, or giving in retirement while minimizing the tax burden. Whether young, old, W-2 employee, or business owner, everyone can benefit from the principles in *More Wealth, Less Taxes*, regardless of where they are currently in their financial planning journey.

-**John Wright**, Entrepreneur

MORE WEALTH, LESS TAXES

Practical, Time-Tested Strategies
to Keep More of What You Earn
and Build Tax-Efficient Wealth
for the Future

LANCE BELLINE CFP®, ChFC®

NEW YORK

LONDON • NASHVILLE • MELBOURNE • VANCOUVER

MORE WEALTH, LESS TAXES

Practical, Time-Tested Strategies to Keep More of What You Earn and Build
Tax-Efficient Wealth for the Future

Published in New York, New York, by Morgan James Publishing. Morgan James is a
trademark of Morgan James, LLC. www.MorganJamesPublishing.com

Proudly distributed by Ingram Publisher Services.

Morgan James BOGO™

A **FREE** ebook edition is available for you
or a friend with the purchase of this print book.

CLEARLY SIGN YOUR NAME ABOVE

Instructions to claim your free ebook edition:
1. Visit MorganJamesBOGO.com
2. Sign your name CLEARLY in the space above
3. Complete the form and submit a photo
   of this entire page
4. You or your friend can download the ebook
   to your preferred device

ISBN 9781631958526 paperback
ISBN 9781631958533 ebook
Library of Congress Control Number:
2021951942

Cover Design by:
Christopher Kirk
www.GFSstudio.com

Interior Design by:
Chris Treccani
www.3dogcreative.net

Morgan James is a proud partner of Habitat for Humanity Peninsula
and Greater Williamsburg. Partners in building since 2006.

Get involved today! Visit MorganJamesPublishing.com/giving-back

TABLE OF CONTENTS

Foreword		*xvii*
Acknowledgments		*xxi*
Introduction		*xxv*
CHAPTER ONE	Everything You Need to Know to Build Wealth Tax-Efficiently	1
	Bird's Eye View	2
	Pool Party	4
	Where Should I Save So I Pay Fewer Taxes Over My Lifetime?	8
	All Are Welcome	9
	How Do I Get Started With the Bucket Strategy?	10
	Don't Put All Your Eggs in One Bucket	11
CHAPTER TWO	Dirty Little Secret #1—How Most People End Up in Bucket One	15
	Instant Gratification	16
	The Government's Raw Deal	17
	Inheritance Taxation	21
	Control Your Taxable Income ... Control Your Taxes ... Give to Charities	22

CHAPTER THREE	When to Plan and When to Pay—Bucket Two	25
	Accumulation Phase	27
	King of Liquidity	27
	Profound Impact: Justin and Brooke Marshall	28
	The Marshalls' Projected Bucket Strategy with Planning	28
	Early Strategic Planning—Ryan and Logan Underwood	30
	The Knipple Ripple	32
	Stars Aligning	33
CHAPTER FOUR	Positive Cash Flow, Tax-Free—Bucket Three	37
	History of Bucket Three Investments	38
	Conversion Law Change	41
	Shut the Front Door	41
	Mega Backdoor	42
	Cash Value Life Insurance	43
	Deferring Gratification—Pay Taxes Now So You Can Pay Less Later	45
	The Switch: David Baskin	46
	Ralph Panek—From Stressed to Blessed	47
	It's Never Too Late (or Too Early) to Take Back Control	49
	Alec Tahy—Motivated by Momentum	50
	Putting It All Together	51
	What Happens if Tax Laws Change?	52
	So, That's the Bucket Strategy. What Next?	52

CHAPTER FIVE   Roadblocks to Wealth Accumulation-The Human
               Element   55
               Mowing for Millions: The Dylan
               Radcliffe Story   56
               The Cost of Convenience   58
               The $10,000 Coke   59
               Bring Back the Lunch Box   60
               Talking Finances—Why Saving and
               Investing Should Be Part of the
               Discussion With Your Kids   60
               John & Karen–Teaching Generational
               Wealth   65
               Small Business Owner or Corporate
               Executive?   69

CHAPTER SIX   Small Business & Corporate Executive Strategies 71
               Small Business Strategies   71
               The Most Important Decision You Will
               Make as a Small Business Owner   72
               Learning & Earning Young: Paying Your
               Children to Work in Your Business   75
               Making Business Pleasurable   76
               Educate Yourself (and then deduct it
               from your taxes)   77
               Retire Confident & Wealthy   78
               Health Plans for Retirement   79
               Bonus, Restricted Stock Units and
               Restricted Stock Options Strategies   81

Supplemental WHAT? Tom E's Story
(New Walmart Exec Client)   82
When to Sell My Restricted Stock or
Restricted Stock Options?   83
To Defer or Not to Defer   85
Maximizing Your 401(k)   86
Health Savings Accounts (HSA)   88

CHAPTER SEVEN   Estate Planning & Charitable Strategies   91
Estate Planning (The Basics)   92
What Happens if I Die Without a Will?   92
Who Takes Care of Your Children if
You Die Without a Will?   92
What is Probate?   93
Benefits of a Will   93
Benefits of a Revocable Trust   94
Family Love Letter   98
Beneficiary Audit   99
Charitable Giving Strategies   100
Gifting Highly Appreciated Stock   101
Donor-Advised Fund   101
Family Foundation   102

CHAPTER EIGHT   Retirement Income of the Future   105
Dividend Stocks vs. Bonds   106
Asymmetric vs. Symmetric Risk   109
Dividends 101   111
22-Year Case Study   111

Just the Facts: Education About the
Market and Investing 115
Intra-Year Declines vs. Calendar Year
Returns 115
Bulls vs. Bears 116
Normal Volatility 116
The Market is Rarely Average 117

CHAPTER NINE A Financial Advisor's Real Value 119
To Behave or Not to Behave 119
Roofing Your House 123
The Foolish Act of Market Timing 125
Thoughts to Control Your Emotions
With Investing 126
Finding the Best Financial Advisor
for Your Family 127
Luis Strohmeier—More Than Just a
Financial Advisor 127
A Life and a Living: Lindsey Pruitt 130
Younger Me: What I Would Have
Done Differently 132
Finishing Well 133
In Closing 135

Glossary of Financial Terms 137
Disclosure 143
About the Author 149

FOREWORD

met Lance in the late 1990s. I was just getting started with my CPA practice, and he was growing his financial practice by talking to business owners about proper insurance coverage. As with most businesses starting out, I could just barely afford basic coverage and bought most of it through my wife's insurance plan with her employer.

Those days remind me how most of us are under-insured … and how we're generally *under-funded* for everything life throws at us. No matter what stage of life, most people play their financial game from behind, in a deficit. With taxes, where people ask for my help, they're always looking for the most <u>immediate</u> way to pay the <u>lowest</u> amount.

I can't blame anyone for wanting to pay the minimum legal amount to the government. It's not like you get much in return for what you pay. But over the years, as Lance and I have worked to develop the Bucket Strategy, one thing's become abundantly clear: Less doesn't always necessarily equal better. For reasons that will become clear as you read, I'm going to give you one broad-ranging answer about how much you should pay in taxes: It depends!

A few years after we met, Lance contacted me about partnering with him to do holistic financial planning for my clients. As a CPA, I've seen partnerships fail for various reasons. Most of the time, they have to do with the quality of relationships and communication between partners. I was uncomfortable at first, going into business with someone I hardly knew. But like a good chess strategist, Lance was patient, optimistic, and willing to walk through the lengthy conversations that led to our partnership. After a year of getting to know him, I decided we could be better together, and provide a more holistic approach to meeting our clients' financial needs.

That year of back-and-forth revealed the things I most appreciate about Lance. He is a man of integrity with strong ethics and morals. He's been determined to do the right thing for my clients since Day One, and has never deviated from that principle. More and more, I'm firmly convinced he wants to do the same good for you through this book. Of course, that isn't to say our journey has been a "perfect" ride (nothing ever is), but I've seen over and over how he handles each client's plan in a customized manner that helps them make the right choices, in their own best interests.

For Lance, the Bucket Strategy is more than a financial tool. It's a system that gives you a glimpse into how he thinks about *everything*. From years of observation, I've noticed how interested he is in *people*, more than he is in managing their money. He wants to understand your story—what lies behind you, where you currently are, and what you hope for and dream of doing tomorrow.

Our financial assets often tell a story different than our aspirations. They're complicated by cultural and family-of-origin stories, and the behaviors we take on in response to them. I've seen Lance wade gently into those issues and help people learn to counteract their own fears and anxieties around money, writing small checks to the IRS while keeping, giving, and passing on their wealth to the people they love the most.

No one can go back and undo the past, but Lance is at his best when assessing where you are in the present and where you want to go in the future. That's a critical reason we work together —so that there's no "guessing" involved in how or whether your money will be taxed. At that point, it becomes a much simpler question: "How can we keep your tax bill in retirement as low as possible, without running afoul of moral, ethical, or legal questions?"

It's a question Lance takes pleasure in answering, and this book provides the tried and tested strategy for getting there.

Here's to your success!
–Travis Riggs, CPA

ACKNOWLEDGMENTS

When I first had the idea to write this book, I honestly felt like it was impossible. It was too daunting of a task, like running a marathon. To be perfectly honest with you, I am not gifted scholastically. Just ask my family; I'm their favorite opponent when we play Trivial Pursuit because they know they'll win and get a good laugh at my expense. I wasn't voted "most likely to succeed" in high school. I had a below-average GPA from the University of Arkansas, and no clue what I wanted to do with my life.

I was surprised to discover that God had his hand on me. He opened doors for me to enter the financial services industry, and gave me a passion for learning, working, succeeding, and failing at one thing for many years. Eventually, I became really good at it. God gave me my purpose to help people gain financial peace of mind and clarity over their financial goals, and I give Him all the credit.

In addition, this book would not have been possible without the counsel, guidance, and inspiration from so many of the great people He's brought into my life. I can't thank them enough for the impact they've made. I am so grateful to have them.

Jessica, my awesome wife who supported my vision to write this book, endured many weekends alone and never complained. She patiently listened to my ideas, and lovingly read the first draft of each chapter. She gave me input that I was looking for, from someone not interested in finance. I knew if I could write it in a way that she could understand and find interesting, then I could accomplish my goal. This book would not exist without her compassion as a wife and mother to my kids.

The B's, my children, thank you for your love and support, and for inspiring me every day to become a better father and a man.

Bruce and Sharon Belline, my parents, have loved me unconditionally and have always been there for me during my personal trials. You have always had my back. I am so grateful. You have also been by my side to celebrate the wins and have been my biggest cheerleaders! Thank you for all your efforts and focus on keeping "Team Belline" so close and instilling in us how important family is.

To my Camma and Trevor, my siblings, with whom I have experienced so many great memories: You both inspire me to become a better person. I love living life with you!

Thank you to Equitable Advisors senior leadership: David Karr, Jim Mellin, MJ Bonadonna, Chris Noonan, and Jeff Moore for supporting me and providing counsel. Also, thanks to my compliance liaison, Rafael Perez-Mendez, for all the work you put in reading and reviewing. I know your plate was already full. I can't tell you how thankful I am for you being willing to take on this additional project.

My study group members, Rich Stewart, Charlie Stanton, Luis Strohmeier, Tim Mason, Kyle Schiffler, and Dallas George—Thank you for always being so open to sharing ideas and best practices. You all contributed in significant ways to make me the financial professional I am today. This book wouldn't have happened without your inspiration. I am a better person because of each of you. Iron sharpens iron!

I am forever grateful to my partners and team members at Lighthouse Financial, who allowed me the extended time away from work to start and finish this project. I love each and every one of you!

My partner Travis Riggs, with whom I've had the privilege to work for over 20 years: You've patiently endured so many of my shortcomings and extended me grace when I didn't deserve it. Thank you for your shared vision to strive for excellence, and never being content with average. I would not be the businessperson I am today without you, and Lighthouse would not be the firm it is today. I look forward to many more years of impacting people's lives with you, my friend.

To all my clients who have trusted me to guide and direct your financial planning, I promise you I don't take it lightly, and I am very thankful. It has been such an amazing experience living life with you. Thank you for the opportunity to live my dream every day. I am indebted to my clients who took the time to share their life experiences for this book. May your stories inspire others and change their lives.

Blake Brewer, thank you for your referral to Paul Edwards, which allowed me to begin this adventure. Paul, you are a stud and gifted individual. It was a pleasure working with your team for sure, and a special shout out to Rebecca Freshour for sharing my vision and the many long hours you shared with me to make this book a reality.

Michael Lieberman, Chapter 8 would never have been possible without you. Thank you for the time you spent with me doing research and helping develop some of the graphics used to articulate the story and benefits of dividend stocks. You are a true professional!

Derek Champagne and the entire team at The Artist Evolution: Your marketing efforts that allowed this book to reach people were an incredible experience, and I really enjoyed partnering with you.

Morgan James, my publisher: This would never have happened without your buy-in and support. David Hancock, I wish you and your entire team many great years to come. You are a true professional.

Darren Thornberry, my editor, thank you so much for making this book read the way it does and making me look much better than I am. I look forward to celebrating with you soon at your favorite watering hole—Odd13 in Lafayette, Colorado.

Don't Swim Upstream to be Financially Independent

———

Have you ever watched a documentary on how salmon swim upstream? It's a perfect picture of how most people think and feel about financial independence. Whether young or approaching retirement, self-employed, or building a career, it seems like an exhausting upstream battle. The rushing water could be compared with the non-stop flow of information, contradicting opinions, and the jargon financial professionals use. And then there's a giant grizzly bear—the Internal Revenue Service (IRS)—rambling along the financial riverbanks, if you will, in America, always looking for an easy meal to satisfy his appetite.

Wild animals have their drawbacks. Fish aren't bright enough to know how to swim as far away from the riverbanks as possible. They not only swim upstream, but they also compete against *other* fish who are doing the same thing. In the same way, most people simply charge through life from a financial standpoint, trying to get to the spawning area (retiring wealthy) at all costs. Some of them get picked off or at least injured when the bear takes a swipe at them.

The grizzly isn't all that bright, either. He doesn't think about building a net or a boat. He's a scavenger, walking up to the edge of the water and grabbing whatever he can. Part of this comes from how he's created; he doesn't understand fishing the way human beings do. When he's not scrounging up food from the riverbank, he goes looking for it in trash cans or campsites. He can definitely kill you ... but he's not much of a predator, like a lion or a cheetah. The IRS is the same way; it's enormous and can maul you, but it doesn't usually come after you unless you swim too close to the riverbanks.

For the first 15 years of my career as a financial advisor, I, like most of my peers, stayed in my lane. I'd develop financial plans, keep clients on track to meet their goals, and make sure they were adequately insured with the correct type of policies. There's nothing wrong with any of that, but I felt conflicted because I wanted to do more. I wanted something that would have a more significant impact and help clients gain <u>real</u> momentum. I didn't just want people to reach their financial goals and survive ... I wanted them to thrive, to look back and see a night-and-day difference in their financial lives.

After a while, I realized that the real impact I could make for clients is to help them reduce or eliminate the amount of wealth they pay to the IRS. For the average American family seeking to become financially independent, pass on generational wealth and maintain their standard of living into old age, the IRS is their most expensive bill and with the lowest return on investment. If all you listen to is pop culture or the media, you might think an abundance of money solves everything. The truth is, if you suddenly get your hands on any sizable sum of it, your first question should be, "How much of this is actually *mine*?" We forget that even pop culture itself once warned, "More money, more problems." For our clients, it's even more specific: <u>Uncle Sam wants his share based on the law</u>, and he's built a vast, complex machine to make sure he gets it.

This is one reason I joined forces with my business partner of over 20 years, Travis Riggs. Travis is a CPA, and we agreed that the models we saw for advising and accounting are inefficient. We wanted to work together so we could be <u>proactive</u> with tax planning AND financial decisions.[1] All financial decisions have a tax implication, whether positive or negative. It makes sense to consider your tax strategy from *every* conceivable angle.

I love working with individuals who have a heightened understanding of money's actual value. They don't look to it as their savior, but they do want to be generous with the blessings they've received. That's the kind of relationship with money that fueled my interest in becoming a Certified Financial Planner (CFP®) professional. I wanted to help people go from "good to great" as *stewards* of their

---

[1]   For more information about our business practices, please see the Disclosure section at the end of the book.

wealth. Along the way, it became clear that the biggest obstacle to their success was—you guessed it—the taxman.

Around age 37, I got tired of scouring the internet and the avalanche of opinions in the financial world. As I encountered other financial advisors through networking, it dawned on me that we are a "lone wolf" class of professionals. Many advisors spend their careers in "grind" mode, trying to figure things out independently. They read endless books and articles and try to anticipate shifts in the market ... without much to show for it. Or they throw their hands up in frustration with the media's nonstop chatter, trying to overcome the "follow the herd" mentality and clients' behavioral biases that inhibit wealth creation. In my opinion most financial professionals themselves get fed a steady diet of malnourished advice from the financial industry and the companies they represent. They're discouraged from thinking outside the box.

I decided I would no longer run my business isolated from the input of fellow financial professionals, especially if their clients were enjoying more success than mine. I was determined to partner with other advisors to find ways to "turn that frown upside down" when their customers dodged colossal tax bills. I reached out to other CFP®s I knew who were geographically remote from one another in places like L.A., Seattle, Denver, Minneapolis, and Nashville.

We began to meet regularly and the tradition continues to this day. Through our conversations over the years, I improved how we ran our advisory firm from top to bottom. If you've heard the saying, "Many hands make light work," you could say I discovered the psychological parallel. The presence of multiple minds makes it far easier to solve complex problems or devise winning strategies. And it wasn't long before Rich Stewart, one of the members, presented the strategy I wanted for my clients: keeping more of your wealth while legally and ethically avoiding high tax rates in retirement.

The Secret Sauce: The Ripple Effect

We were at our annual five-day meeting in Breckenridge, Colorado, one year when Rich stood up in front of the whiteboard and wrote, "Withdrawing money from your IRA and not paying taxes." I thought to myself, "*That isn't possible.*"

He followed it up with "how to live on $100,000 and pay no taxes." In one of those "eureka" moments, I found myself doing a double-take and saying, "Wait a minute ... say that again?" And when Rich spelled it out one more time, I realized I wasn't dreaming. I'd just struck gold. Have you ever had a moment in your life where you learned something so obvious, you were a little embarrassed that you failed to think of it? Rich called this strategy "The Ripple Effect," and I felt ashamed that I'd never thought of it.

I left that meeting with a slate of questions for Travis, my partner. When I told him what I'd learned, repeating what Rich had said, he was skeptical. We spent hours going through different "what if" tax returns until the light bulb went on for him ... and the Bucket Strategy was formed.

There are two ways to think about Rich's "Ripple Effect." The first could be compared to ripples in water, as when an object like a boat creates a wake. If you were to visit Beaver Lake, not far from where I live, you could observe how the ripple waves from speedboats spread across the water. Eventually, those ripples affect other objects (or critters, like ducks) sitting on the surface of the water. Buoys, slower boats, kayaks, and canoes take turns getting a "bump" as the waves pass underneath them.

Financially, this means that in retirement, controlling or reducing the amount of taxable income from <u>one</u> source can spike or increase the tax rates you pay in another. In the same way, a speedboat pushes *down* on the water as it goes. The water on either side of the boat bulges and spreads outward. The closer you are to the wake, the more you can expect to be impacted by it.

The other way to look at the Ripple Effect is with <u>distance</u>. If you see a boat approaching in the distance, you can navigate to be as far from its wake as possible. The same is true with the Internal Revenue Code. The Code tends to punish those who fail to plan in advance of retirement with higher income taxes. These people drift too close to the wake made by the boat. And most of the time, the "drifters" are people who don't have very good "water navigation skills" in advance of retirement. They don't see the taxman coming because they're too focused on other priorities. It's usually too late once they've retired and started drawing income from their savings and filing tax returns. This was the lesson of the Ripple Effect—chart your course <u>far away</u>, in advance of the IRS' wake as it passes by every spring, and you end up with more money in your pocket and fewer taxes to pay.

So, I now give you the keys to the kingdom: *More Wealth, Less Taxes.*

The good news is that no matter how big the IRS gets, it doesn't have a monopoly on financial literacy. It doesn't hire CPAs and CFP®s with years of experience consulting with clients. Even the congressional committees who write the tax code fail to foresee the loopholes they create by writing their laws in the first place. There is far too much one-dimensional thinking among legislative and bureaucratic bodies to truly "rob" you of your money the way it's portrayed in the media.

Unless there's a complete revolutionary overhaul of society, you have little to fear about the government's behavior in the long term. On one cable network, the media screams about "the rich not paying their fair share," and a few channels away, they panic about "tax rates going up." That may be a problem locally if your state has an unfriendly business climate. But as far as the federal government goes, you've got very little to fear. They're far too concerned ideologically with appearing on the side of "the little guy." If you know how to arrange your money in "buckets" so that on paper you <u>appear</u> to them as a little guy in retirement, there isn't much they can do about it. It's legal, honest, and entirely at your discretion.

We call this approach "The Bucket Strategy," which shows you how to build wealth strategically, so you can keep, endow and transfer your wealth to people and causes you care about instead of giving it to the IRS in retirement. We've used it for the past decade with all of our clients. It is the point of reference for each meeting we hold. It's the ultimate "filter" for you to fund a lifestyle of financial independence. It equips you to write checks to churches, causes, and charities. It blazes a trail for you to leave an inheritance to your children's children, if you do it the right way for a sufficient length of time. Our clients get the answer to the most crucial question we all ask ourselves: *How do I put myself in the position to become financially independent without setting myself up to pay a fortune in taxes later?"*

When you finish this book, you should be able to:

- Learn strategies that allow you to pay less in taxes in retirement, give more to charities and transfer more wealth to your loved ones.
- Get a clear, 30,000-foot view of your finances and a workable road map to keep more, give generously, plan your estate and pay fewer taxes.
- Learn common mistakes you must avoid that inhibit the amount of wealth you accumulate.
- Identify how your money is allocated in each bucket and the projected future value of each based on your current savings strategy vs. strategic saving.

- If you're a business owner, learn strategies to grow your wealth more tax efficiently.
- If you work for a company, better utilize your company benefits.
- Know what questions to ask when interviewing a financial professional or financial firm.

And, of course, if you reach the end and want to discuss taking this journey together, we'll have links and resources you can follow to contact our office.

Wishing you every success on the journey!
Lance Belline

CHAPTER ONE

Everything You Need to Know to Build Wealth Tax-Efficiently

———

*"Many caterpillars defend themselves not by striking fear in the
hearts of their predators, but rather indifference.
The large maple spanworm looks like a twig; the viceroy
caterpillar looks like a bird dropping.
This isn't as exciting as looking like an anaconda, but when you
are very small, and wingless, one of your main goals in life is to
not be exciting."*

- Amy Leach

*"I went to buy some camouflage trousers the other day,
but I couldn't find any."*

- Tommy Cooper

So … what would you think about the idea of retiring
on $120,000 a year with an annual tax rate of just
1.18 percent?

You'd probably start out wondering … "Is that legal? It sounds too good to be true." When something sounds too good to be true, it usually is. I hear you … but I'm not kidding. Read on.

Bird's Eye View

To better understand the concept, it's a good idea to get a bird's eye view of the Bucket Strategy at work, as though you were flying over a vast outdoor pool with three dividers running parallel from one end to the other. These three lanes represent your retirement assets: Bucket One, Bucket Two, and Bucket Three.

The first lane, **Bucket One**, comprises what the IRS calls **ordinary income**. This is the category it watches closely for collection purposes. In 2022, tax rates range from 10 to 37 percent, with five brackets in between. The more you earn in Bucket One, the higher your tax rate. Bucket One's gainfully employed people of working age with W-2 or self-employed income are generally subject to the prying eyes of the IRS. But there's another category from which the IRS receives a lot of its revenue: retirees withdrawing money from their pre-tax retirement accounts, like traditional IRAs. Sadly, if you spent your career accumulating wealth in Bucket One, there's very little we can do to reduce the amount of money you'll pay to the IRS when you retire, based on current tax law. But in other stories, you'll see how we work within the law to help people keep far more of their nest egg than they thought possible.

The IRS looks differently at the money you earn from the second lane, or **Bucket Two.** If I had to give it a name, I'd call it **passive income** because the IRS has many categories—capital gains, real estate income, dividends from stocks, and so forth. You earn this money mainly as an *investor* rather than as an employee. Uncle Sam has three tax rates for this money currently: zero, 15, and 20 percent. Your tax rate in Bucket Two is determined from the amount you earn from your job, business or what you withdraw from Bucket One in retirement. In 2022, if your Bucket One income is $83,550 or less, you qualify for the zero percent tax rate in Bucket Two. If you earn over $83,550, but less than $647,850, you pay 15 percent taxes in Bucket Two. If you earn over $647,850, you pay 20 percent. If you're just starting out, or still have many working years left on the clock, this is a great reason to start investing. If you're older or close to retirement, a full Bucket Two can be handy and beneficial.

The third lane, or **Bucket Three**, is tax-free income and one of the best things Congress ever did for the American people to allow them to accumulate for retirement. In 1997, they passed the Taxpayer Relief Act, signed by President Bill Clinton. The author of the bill was Senator William Roth of Delaware. In a bold, preventative move, Roth's bill created an **income savings category** that accumulates without being taxed in the future. The most famous product to come out of this is the Roth IRA, where you invest after-income tax money and allow it to grow tax-free. I will go into more detail about other investments in this category in Chapter 4.

Pool Party

Let's go back to the swimming pool. As you fly overhead and look closer, using your sharp eagle eyes, you notice all the swimmers in lane one are swimming above the surface, easily seen by the lifeguards. Some freestyle, others backstroke, breaststroke, or butterfly. Lane one is the busiest and narrowest lane; it is *packed*, whereas the other two have much more room. Few people in lane one ever leave it. Either they can't because all their retirement assets are in Bucket One, they don't know *how* (no one taught them), or maybe they were told they need to be there (by their financial professional). Who knows? The point is, most of them stay.

You notice several lifeguards (representing the IRS) focusing most of their attention on the swimmers in lane one. Through their peripheral vision, they also watch the swimmers in lane two. They're busy blowing their whistles at the swimmers and not allowing them to have fun. They completely ignore lane three.

Lane two, meanwhile, has a fair amount of traffic. It's one hundred times wider than lane one, however, giving swimmers a lot more room. You notice most of the swimmers in lane two are snorkeling, spending much of their time underwater, surfacing for a short time, and then going back under. The lifeguards have a tough time keeping track of them. Sometimes, the swimmers go over to lane one, and sometimes they hang out in lane three, but neither for very long. The lifeguards sometimes blow their whistles at the swimmers in lane two, but definitely not as often or as loud. Lane two is like Bucket Two—still taxable, but it has tremendous advantages over Bucket One in retirement.

Lane three is the "pool party lane." Even though it's not as big as lane two, it has about the same amount of traffic. It's more relaxed and fun. People of every age group are in it. Kids run and jump freely off the deck and into the water, splashing the adults, who simply smile and laugh along. Young adults are up on the deck, playing the cabana music, swimming up to the bar, and ordering margaritas. Middle-aged and older adults take turns sunning themselves and getting into the water to cool off. The athletic swimmers are also there, taking laps if they feel like it. Some are just there for the party and the scene; they barely get in the water at all. The lifeguards ignore them and let them do whatever they want.

Then you notice something else: figures moving <u>underneath</u> the water on the surface. You zoom in closer and realize they are swimmers *below* the waterline. They might be scuba divers or snorkelers, or even Navy SEALs training to see how long they can hold their breath. It's only now that you realize the people beneath the water swim in any direction they please. The lanes don't seem to apply to them. How deep is this pool, anyway? Is it a diving tank? You begin to follow the patterns of the underwater swimmers, and you notice that most of them surface in all three lanes.

These swimmers rarely surface in lane one. Only one or two of them do, and only for the briefest moment before they dive back under. They are equipped with plenty of oxygen to breathe, wetsuits to keep warm, and goggles to see clearly. They don't need as much air as the other swimmers. Some of them never surface in lane one; they only come up in the other two lanes. The swimmers living in lanes two and three are the winners at the Bucket Strategy. Their extended families can join them in lanes two and three because they've paid the admission price for the people they love instead of giving it to the control-freak lifeguards (the IRS).

If you're starting to grasp the fundamentals of the strategy, let me illustrate and validate the statement at the beginning of the chapter ... living on $120,000 of income a year and only paying 1.18 percent in taxes.

	PRE-TAX BUCKET EARNED, TAXABLE 401(k), IRA INCOME (QUALIFIED PLAN DISTRIBUTIONS)	AFTER-TAX BUCKET CAPITAL GAINS	TAX FREE BUCKET ROTH IRA, LIFE INSURANCE POLICY, CASH VALUE LOAN PROCEEDS*
Funds withdrawn	$40,000	$40,000	$40,000
Standard or itemized deductions	-$25,900		
Taxable Income	$14,100		
Estimated Federal Tax	$1,410	- 0 -	- 0 -

You're retired! You made it! You no longer collect a W-2 from your employer or business. Here's how we get your income of $120,000 while you pay only $1,410 in taxes.

You withdraw $40,000 from each bucket.

Bucket One money is your taxable income. It's like your W-2 income when you were working, but once you subtract the standard deduction ($25,900), your taxable income goes from $40K to $14,100.

By having a taxable income of $14,100, you fly well below the lowest 12 percent tax bracket of $83,500 for Bucket Two, which means the $40K you withdraw from Bucket Two gets taxed at a 0 percent tax rate. You don't have to be great at math to determine that equals zero!

Bucket Three is never taxed, so you withdraw $40K tax-free.

That means you pay the absolute lowest rate of 10 percent in federal taxes on your taxable income of $14,100, which is $1,410!

Where Should I Save So I Pay Fewer Taxes Over My Lifetime?

This is the question you should ask yourself, instead of "How do I pay fewer taxes this calendar year?" I don't mean you *totally* ignore trying to pay fewer taxes, but we've been trained by society to make this our primary focus without thinking about the long-term effects. The Bucket Strategy is not complicated once you learn it, but it does take concentration in the short term and commitment in the long term. When you think of money this way, you have to be able to see things that *don't currently exist.* It's a cruel thing to experience the sting of owing tens or hundreds of thousands of dollars to Uncle Sam every time you need to pay a large bill in retirement, especially when you're well past your prime earning years.

If you save strategically and steward your wealth well, then not only will you benefit in your retirement years by paying less in taxes, but your wealth will also transfer more tax-efficiently to your children or heirs.

Here are two other benefits of the Bucket Strategy:

1. **You can save less each year** because you won't need to accumulate as big of a nest egg since you are paying less federal tax in retirement.

2. **You save the same amount,** but live on more money during retirement or give more away to friends, family, and charities.

Regardless of your age or where you are in your wealth accumulation journey, investing in the Bucket Strategy can help you realize your future financial goals, including more money to live on in retirement, more to give to charity, and more to leave as a financial legacy to your family.

All Are Welcome

The best part about the Bucket Strategy is how it works for <u>both</u> young investors just starting out and people preparing to retire. It works for business owners <u>and</u> highly paid employees. Tactically, it changes shape over time. But one thing that hasn't changed, regardless of who dominates Congress or holds the White House, is that *Uncle Sam will not notice you if you play by the rules and keep your distance.* If you know how to keep the correct percentages of your total assets in non-taxable waters, the government's own laws prohibit them from demanding a share of it. This is how the rich pay less in taxes; you only pay *less* if you *appear* to be poor. The progressive income tax system in place greatly reduces or even eliminates the tax burden on lower-income earners in the first place, which means higher income earners are their primary target. That is, <u>unless the IRS can't see you because you have planned accordingly and have less taxable income to recognize on your yearly tax filing</u>.

How Do I Get Started With the Bucket Strategy?

No matter where you are on the journey, the first step is always to zoom out to 30,000 feet and ask, "Where does my money currently go?" It always goes *somewhere*, even if "somewhere" is an empty coffee can under your mattress or a box buried in your backyard. However, let me add a caveat: Just because you know your money is going into a retirement account today doesn't mean you can calculate what will happen if you wait several decades before withdrawing it. That's why our advisory firm created the Asset Organizer—a spreadsheet you can download at lancebelline.net to view your wealth now and in the future.

Once you fill out the Asset Organizer, you should have a much clearer picture of how much you've accumulated in each bucket. You can forecast your bucket percentages in retirement based on how you're currently saving and compare them to your future percentages if you change your savings strategy. It will help answer one of the most common questions we are asked: "How much should I be saving in each bucket?" This is how to think about "**intelligent wealth**," as my friend and client Rob Schiederer likes to say. Don't get nervous if you've put all your eggs in Bucket One up to this point. The question now becomes, "At what age would you like to become financially independent?" Unless you are already in the traditional "retirement years" and your assets are entirely in Bucket One, there's usually *something* you can do to clip Uncle Sam's wings before he flies off with more of your money. For example, you can turn off the spigot for Bucket One and flood Buckets Two and Three with every penny you can spare.

Don't Put All Your Eggs in One Bucket

This is probably the most widely known principle for investing. Regardless of investing experience, people generally know they should not invest 100 percent of their money in one stock or mutual fund. Instead, they choose from several sources and keep a diverse portfolio. So I ask you: Why don't you apply this principle to your savings strategy? Why are you saving all your eggs in Bucket One for retirement? If you do, you become 100 percent dependent on whatever future tax rates are when you retire. I don't know about you, but I don't like being completely dependent on anyone—*especially* our government. I don't have a crystal ball about the future of tax rates, but take a look at the following tax timeline that shows the history of the highest income and capital gain tax rates.

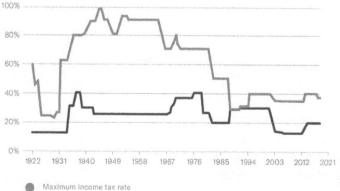

Historically speaking, the tax rates since the late 1990s have been some of the lowest. Plenty of intelligent economists say tax rates will have to be higher in the future to fund our national debt. It's just common sense. *The government will have to cut spending or increase revenue, or a combination of the two.* But history proves that our elected officials don't like to cut government subsidy programs, especially when campaigning for re-election. If taxes drift higher in the future, then a person currently saving in Bucket One is saving taxes in a low tax rate environment and will be making withdrawals in a higher tax rate environment. Why would you want to do that?

The Bucket Strategy is a "divide and conquer" plan of attack so that you can have greater influence on how your income is taxed in retirement. To accomplish this, you must be willing to pay a little more tax now and even see less net income, which could affect your lifestyle spending. But I have found—and the client stories in this book illustrate—that you're unlikely to notice these drawbacks. By making these small sacrifices today, you position yourself to have a say about how much tax you pay in the future. Regardless of future tax rates and rules, having a diversified portfolio in the three buckets will allow you the most flexibility to take advantage of future tax rates.

An old proverb says, "The best time to plant a tree is twenty years ago. The second best time is now." I believe the same holds true for saving and investing your money strategically. If today's your first day thinking this way, great! And if you've already been at it for a while, but you want to keep, give and pass on more wealth to your heirs, that's even better. In the following chapters, we will go into more detail about investment options in each bucket and how to optimize them. You'll read stories of how we've done this for our clients, along with principles and steps you can follow to more wealth and fewer taxes.

CHAPTER TWO

Dirty Little Secret #1—How Most People End Up in Bucket One

———

"The ability to discipline yourself to delay gratification in the short term in order to enjoy the greater rewards in the long term is the indispensable prerequisite for success."

Brian Tracy

"If you don't want to be average, don't rush into doing what the crowd is doing."

- Constance Chuks Friday

For my first decade as a certified financial planner, I spent way too much time running in circles in Bucket One. Most of my clients did, too. Most Americans hope Social Security and 401(k) plans will save the day when they're in the late stages of life. Putting your financial fate in the hands of the government won't give you the results you want. The problem is when we assume they have our best interests at heart. I've learned the hard way:

Just because somebody isn't out to hurt you doesn't mean they're out to help you, either.

The government has good reasons to offer you a tax break for Bucket One investments. They want to take advantage of the "Rule of 72," just like anyone else.[2] The government knows your investments grow over time, and they're happy to forgo a small chunk of it now to get a much bigger one later on.

> EXAMPLE:
> You put $10,000 in your 401(k) before taxes.
> Assuming a 20 percent tax rate, Uncle Sam passes up on $2,000 of revenue.
> Over the next few decades, your $10K grows to $100K. When you retire, Uncle Sam collects $20,000 in taxes as you withdraw.

See how this works? The government thinks the same way you do about growing your nest egg. The only difference is *they're not working for it*, which makes it a shame they get more of your money.

Instant Gratification

People on both sides of the argument over taxes are much less divided regarding the immediate gratification of keeping their money. Would you choose to save on your

---

2   The "Rule of 72" is a quick formula you can use to calculate how long it will take you to double your money, based on the return you earn each year. More on this in the Glossary.

taxes now or in 30 years? It is human nature to want to pay fewer taxes now. That's usually how the government and culture present the choice with 401(k) and traditional retirement accounts.

The Bucket Strategy requires a mindset shift. Society has conditioned us to think the government offers these "breaks" because of moral conscience and empathy. It's fine to believe the best about people, but you're in trouble if you think it's the *only* reason. Considering how often politicians level the charge at the private sector for being obsessed with "profits over people," you have to scratch your head at how consistently they show up to demand a cut of your money. It sounds weird until you consider that the math supports it: When you opt into a traditional retirement account, it's *the government* that defers gratification. That goes against the idea we hear in the media that our government is not good at delaying gratification!

The Government's Raw Deal

Pre-tax retirement plans grew in popularity after the Employee Retirement Income Security Act (ERISA) of 1974. Gradually, as tax laws changed in the 1980s, they became more widely available, and contribution limits increased. Initially, they were a response to some key financial collapses of the 1960s, where plants and firms closed down and people's pension benefits disappeared. Up until the late 1990s, plans like traditional IRAs, 401(k), and deferred comp were the best you could hope for unless your employer maintained a conventional pension plan.

Some of our clients discovered that ERISA caused them as many problems as it solved. Individuals could now build their wealth accounts without depending on their employer to stay in business and fund pensions. They could enter retirement with plenty of money to live on. But the bigger their retirement accounts grew, the more the IRS wanted in taxes for the privilege of using it. A major concern with putting your money in pre-tax retirement accounts is this: **You are 100 percent exposed to future income tax rates.**

Henry and Grace moved their portfolio to our firm after a long, disappointing season where they lost a lot of money. When we looked at their situation, we saw that they had 90 percent of their retirement funds in Bucket One. Fortunately, they still had enough to provide a comfortable retirement income, but not without paying thousands of dollars to the IRS every time they made a significant purchase. If they wanted to spend $20,000 to remodel their deck, we'd tell them to withdraw $27,000 ... because of taxes. If they needed a new $10,000 roof on their home, we'd tell them to withdraw $14,000. Henry told me, "I always feel like I'm getting taken for a ride. I can never get the upper hand on Uncle Sam." Henry doesn't have to go back to work; they have enough to survive and pay their bills. It's just that they worked very hard, for many years, to save all the money they did. They did this *so that* they could experience more freedom and good things in retirement.

Some people lean on pre-tax plans like deferred comp because they don't trust themselves to save their excess income when it's deposited into their checking account. Or they want to hide income from their (spender) spouses. If you are inclined to spend money merely because you have it, or you're married to a spender, yes, your money *does* get saved (which is better than not saving at all). But if you go that route and those accounts grow like they're supposed to, the IRS is going to ask for its portion. Wouldn't it be better, if you're going to be vigilant over yourself and your spouse, to be vigilant against the government as well?

Another client, Joe, reached age 55 in excellent financial shape. He'd built up his deferred comp plan to pay him an annual income of $250,000 for 15 years. That's more than enough to continue his lifestyle well into retirement. It's a significant income. I know many people who would like to trade places with him. But when you consider the math of what he deferred initially over 20 years and what he "saved" versus what he'll pay in retirement, it's <u>Uncle Sam</u> who's taking in a considerable amount.

Deferred Comp Accumulation (what Joe saved without paying taxes)	Deferred Comp Distribution (what Joe pays in taxes now that he's retired)
$75,000, 40% tax rate[3]	$250,000, 30% tax rate
Annual tax savings $30,000	Annual tax paid $75,000
Total tax savings $600,000	Total tax paid $1,125,000

---

3   The tax rates are for illustrative purposes only and assume a higher tax rate while working than in retirement.

You might look at this and say, "You didn't account for the $30,000 in tax savings he could invest, and what that would have grown to over 15 years!" I agree with the logic, but that's not reality. Most people spend the money! It gets absorbed in lifestyle expenses, just like an annual tax refund. In over 20 years, I have had **one** client who did cash flow budgeting so precise and detailed that he took his tax savings on his 401(k) and invested it rather than spent it.

You could be like Sarah, another client who receives $5,000 per month from an old-school pension plan after 30 years at her company. It's wonderful she gets $60,000 a year to supplement her income, but since Sarah is unmarried, she is above the minimum 12 percent tax bracket in Bucket One. This triggers taxation when she earns dividends or sells her investments in Bucket Two. She must pay another 15 percent in taxes. Had she understood the implications of pension plans, she might not have valued them so much. Her plan forces her to have higher income taxes now. If she'd been strategic with her retirement income, she could probably pay 50 percent less! It's a shame that so much of her money goes to Uncle Sam when it doesn't have to. This situation causes her to surface above the water in lane two, and the IRS lifeguard is very happy to blow the whistle.

It's important to understand—these clients sit on top of vast piles of money. Bucket One retirement plans have helped many individuals accumulate large nest eggs for retirement. The problem with these plans is that the bigger they get, *the more of it is sent to Uncle Sam in the form of income taxes when you withdraw it*, especially if you depend on it for your income when you retire. If you're young and starting your journey, you could compare Bucket One financial products with outdated technology like rotary dial telephones or videocassette recorders. Sure, you can make phone calls and watch movies on them, but your mobility and shareability factors go through the floor. The beauty of the smartphone, meanwhile, is you have all those abilities in your pocket. You can make calls and watch movies wherever and whenever you want and share your joy with friends and family.

Inheritance Taxation

Speaking of friends and family, here's another big downside to Bucket One plans. <u>Your heirs get taxed on them, too</u>! Sadly, if your retirement funds pass to your kids, *they* will have to pay income taxes when they make withdrawals on them as well! And they can't avoid them! The government's rules are that all of your assets in Bucket One have to be entirely distributed by December 31 of the 10th year following your death. Here's an example:

- You leave your kids $1 million in Bucket One.
- To distribute that within 10 years, they will likely take equal distributions of $100K per year. This sounds nice, but …
- … because your kids are usually still in their accumulation years, it can spike THEIR taxable income! If they are making a lot of money and

therefore in a high tax bracket, this 100K just spikes their income even more and the government gets a higher percentage of it.

Control Your Taxable Income ... Control Your Taxes ... Give to Charities

I don't want to sound like a curmudgeon about Bucket One plans. They have many positives, and in retirement they are great for benefiting the charities you care about. Through strategic planning, my clients Richard and Cindy Knipple became significant donors to their church. They wanted to make a six-figure donation while the church was being built. We recommended they withdraw the $100,000 from Richard's IRA and have zero federal or state taxes withheld. This triggered a taxable event, but when he received the money into his checking account, he then wrote a check to the church for $100,000, which qualified for a deductible charitable contribution, thus bringing their taxable income back to $0. We called it their year of "Giving Six, Living Six, and Owing Less Than Six." We withdrew money from their Buckets Two and Three investments for them to live on. Pretty cool to give away six figures, live on six figures and pay less than five percent in federal income taxes.

Another way to get your IRA money to charities is to donate to the charitable organization directly because it avoids recognition as taxable income from the account, keeping your income at $0.[4]

The parallel with taxes is this: They're still a given, but the question of *how much you pay* can be more fluid than you think. Depending on how much runway you have until you reach retirement age, you can build toward financial independence and pay little to no taxes. It is true; you're required to make withdrawals on pre-tax accounts like traditional IRAs after the age of 72. Our team identifies tax burdens like those, especially if there's enough time to convert them into other accounts with a much lighter tax bill. If you can stomach those taxes, commit to a disciplined program, and then spot-check it every few months with an advisor, you'll fly well below the IRS' radar by keeping control of your taxable income in retirement.

Whether or not you have time on your side, there are better places to store and grow your nest egg. In the next chapter, we'll explore the big one—Bucket Two—and how you can use it to go from "working for your money" to "money working for you."

---

4   See more on qualified charitable distribution strategy in the Glossary. Individuals should always consult with their tax professional prior to taking action in relation to any charitable donation strategy.

CHAPTER THREE

When to Plan and When to Pay— Bucket Two

———

"A compass, I learnt when I was surveying, it'll point you true north from where you're standing, but it's got no advice about the swamps and deserts and chasms that you'll encounter along the way. If in pursuit of your destination, you plunge ahead, heedless of obstacles, and achieve nothing more than to sink in a swamp, what's the use of knowing true north?"

- Daniel Day-Lewis, as President Abraham Lincoln in "Lincoln"

Bucket Two assets-income include:

- Your portfolio: dividends and capital gains from stocks, mutual funds, and exchange-traded funds (ETFs).
- Capital gains from corporate, government, and municipal bonds.
- Real estate: rent from tenants or capital gains from the sale of a property.

- Interest income from corporate and government bonds.
- Interest income from money market and savings accounts.

I've come to call Bucket Two your "Decathlon Bucket." Do you watch the Olympics? In my opinion, decathlon athletes are the most versatile and well-rounded athletes on the planet. They are highly competitive in all 10 track and field events. They compete in the 100-meter dash, running long jump, shot put, high jump, 400-meter run, 110-meter hurdles, discus, pole vault, javelin, and 1,500-meter run. Who would you choose if you were a coach and could only take one athlete to a track and field event? Your best decathlon athlete, right? Not your best sprinter or shot put thrower. Those athletes might win one event, but they'd finish last in the other nine.

Bucket Two investments are like decathlon athletes. They allow the most flexibility and offer significant benefits to the strategic investor during all phases of life. Without a strategy, however, you'll pay too much income taxes in both phases of your life. Why do it if you don't have to? This chapter will reveal Bucket Two tools and strategies to keep more of your wealth and potentially pay less to the IRS. First, however, let's focus on how to think about taxes while working versus when you're retired.

Accumulation Phase

The first part of your lifespan with money occurs approximately between ages 18 and 65 and is called the accumulation phase. You are working and saving for different financial goals such as cars, houses, college educations, retirement, etc. I will go out on a limb and recommend *against* trying to qualify for a zero percent tax rate during this long season. This is actually when you want to pay the <u>most</u> taxes. What?! Why would I say that? Well, as I mentioned in Chapter One, in 2022, assuming you're married and filing jointly, your taxable income would have to be below $83,550 to qualify for the zero percent capital gain and dividend tax rate. The likelihood of having excess money to invest after paying your mortgage, car payments, and other family living expenses is low.

On the other hand, if you qualify for the 20 percent capital gains rate, that means your federal taxable income exceeds $647,850. If your income is that high, you should be able to save quite a bit of money, right? So if you fall into this category, give thanks to God above, give generously and invest heavily.

King of Liquidity

Bucket Two investments are essential because they can be used for all your financial goals without penalties, whereas Buckets One and Three are limited to just retirement. When do most of your financial goals occur? Before 59½, you need liquid investments. And what about those unexpected, major expenses that pop up during life? If you're young and reading this and thinking, "I want to retire at 45 or 50," a big Bucket Two will be a big help.

Profound Impact: Justin and Brooke Marshall

Five years or so into their marriage, Justin and Brooke Marshall relocated to northwest Arkansas. We met at my brother's CrossFit box (CrossFit 540, if you are ever in Northwest Arkansas—get a workout with us!).

When they first came to me, they were already well on their way, saving for their financial goals. I showed them how to save strategically and diversify their future wealth using the Bucket Strategy. Below are the initial percentages they started with in each bucket, the projected future values in each bucket with their existing strategy, and the result of changing their savings strategy projected over $500,000 of tax savings in retirement.

The Marshalls' Projected Bucket Strategy with Planning

	Bucket One	Bucket Two	Bucket Three
Initial	77%	23%	0%
Projected w/o planning	55%	45%	0%
Projected with planning	30%	40%	30%

Since our initial meeting seven years ago, the Marshalls' profitable real estate transactions have increased their Bucket Two ratio even more and allowed them to be financially independent in their early 40s.

"Both our families instilled a great work ethic and moral values in us," said Brooke, "but we didn't know what to do with money other than save it and not spend it. We listened to a lot of Dave Ramsey's teachings and funded our 401(k)s ... and that was about it." This shows that many people might have an excellent *attitude* about managing money, but not always the knowledge of how to invest it or where to save it. Justin and Brooke agreed that switching from a pre-tax savings plan to a Roth barely affected them, as far as taxes were concerned. "We haven't noticed any drastic changes to our lifestyle spending over the last ten years. We didn't have to go without buying what we wanted to buy or not spend what we wanted to spend after changing our savings from Bucket One to Bucket Three investments," Justin said. "What caught me off guard was when we reached the point we could begin to live off our investments if we wanted to and the little amount of taxes we would pay. When Brooke told me how much we had, I refused to believe it and had to hear it from Lance directly." (I was happy to confirm that Brooke's calculations were correct).

More importantly, the Marshalls are creating a different legacy for their children than the one they received. They have far more in generational wealth than their parents did. "The kids attend a private, faith-based school," Brooke said. "It's been a privilege and blessing to contribute in a big way to pay raises for teachers, new technology for the school and the church we attend. We had always wanted to be able to give like no one else, and now we do." Without the dividend income from their Bucket Two investments, the Marshalls' age would force them to continue working when they don't have to.

Early Strategic Planning—Ryan and Logan Underwood

Ryan became a client right after he graduated college. His father, Tom, was already a client and asked me to meet with Ryan to help him get off to a great financial start. It wasn't hard. Ryan was already a diligent saver. He was maxing out his 401(k) (Bucket One) working at Walmart, and he started saving in Buckets Two and Three. Fortunately, he met the love of his life, Logan, who was also prudent with her finances. Their primary goal was to be financially independent well before the standard retirement age. We looked at their current bucket mix. With how their savings were allocated in each bucket, retiring before age 60 was out of the question. They could not access their Bucket One assets until then.

"In 2012, Lance started talking about the Bucket Strategy with us," said Ryan. "It's awesome to see where we were then versus where we are now. Based on how it's going, in the next four years, we'll be financially independent. I'll be 41, and Logan will be 40, so we have the rest of our lives ahead of us to spend with our little boy and see him grow up and enjoy life."

"The biggest win from this," says Logan, "is that we'll be able to do whatever we want. Maybe that means still working. Maybe that means volunteering. Maybe it means working a job that we're very passionate about. *It allows us the flexibility to do whatever we want.*"

Ryan and Logan achieved this by changing their saving strategies to meet their early financial independence goal. Based on current goals and projections, they will likely be able to live off their liquid, accessible investments from Buckets Two and Three until they reach retirement age. Below are the initial percentages they started with in each bucket, the projected future values in each bucket with their existing strategy, and the result of changing their savings strategy.

The Underwoods' Projected Bucket Strategy with Planning

	Bucket One	Bucket Two	Bucket Three
Initial	65%	18%	17%
Projected w/o planning	45%	29%	26%
Projected with planning	26%	24%	50%

Distribution Phase

The second part of your lifespan, as it relates to money, is called the distribution phase. This is when we want to position your Bucket Two investments correctly to take advantage of the zero percent tax rate! The following is an example of living off $109,250 in 2022 from qualified dividends and paying ZERO federal income taxes.

	PRE-TAX BUCKET EARNED, TAXABLE 401(k), IRA INCOME (QUALIFIED PLAN DISTRIBUTIONS)	AFTER-TAX BUCKET CAPITAL GAINS	TAX FREE BUCKET ROTH IRA, LIFE INSURANCE POLICY, CASH VALUE LOAN PROCEEDS*
Funds withdrawn	$0	$109,450	$0
Standard or itemized deductions		-$25,900	
Taxable Income		$83,550	
Estimated Federal Tax		- 0 -	

After your standard deduction, you get your taxable income to be equal to the top of the 12 percent income tax bracket, which allows you to qualify for it. Let's do that simple math again! $83.550*0=Zero.

The Knipple Ripple

After 27 years at Kraft Foods, Richard had his sights set on retiring at 55. He'd already worked with another financial professional, and (fortunately), he'd saved aggressively in Bucket Two, which made up 44 percent of his portfolio. "I was 100 percent invested in tobacco stock for 15 years," he said. "I used to tell my old advisor, 'I don't want my retirement to go up in smoke.' He (the advisor) never discussed tax strategies about my investments or how to pay less taxes. I thought people did that through tax write-offs.

I had no idea you could be strategic about your source of income in retirement until I met Lance and Travis."

We flooded Richard's Bucket Three savings in his final five working years and built it up to about 10 percent of his portfolio. In 2012, his last year of work, Richard's salary put him in the top 30 to 35 percent income tax rate. He paid only <u>$11 in taxes</u> while living on a six-digit income in his first full retirement year!

"I'm still making massive contributions to my family, church, and society," said Richard. "I just get to do it without working full-time. One of my nieces totaled her GMC Yukon, so I bought her another one. We helped my daughter buy a house in 2015 after she got married. I bought my son-in-law a new truck as well. Those kids are never completely off the payroll, are they?" he laughed. "I was also able to help both of my sisters and their kids with vehicles, mortgage payments, wisdom teeth removal, physical therapy, you name it. My niece, Summer, was in a terrible car accident with major head injuries. She's continued to live with mental and physical challenges ever since, and we've helped pay off loans and medical bills for her."

Stars Aligning

My client, Brad, "lucked in" to the Bucket Strategy. He started at a young age, saving as much as he could in Bucket Two via his company stock. "After my wife and I had our children, all my focus was on saving. I was like … save, save, save as much as we could." At the time, he was thinking more of *how much* he needed to save instead of *where to save to be tax-efficient in retirement.*

Unfortunately, due to some health issues, Brad had to retire earlier than he expected. Still, he was confident the amount of money he'd acquired would cover the lifestyle he wanted to maintain. He and his wife moved to Northwest Arkansas to be closer to his son and grandchildren. Together with his son, they interviewed firms to manage his retirement and investment portfolios. After they told me they'd chosen ours, I asked, "Why?"

Brad said, "For two reasons. One—you showed you cared about my family, and it was about more than just the money or another account. Two—none of the other firms we interviewed talked about distribution strategies to pay fewer taxes like you did. They discussed managing the money and forecasting how much we could spend and not run out. But not how to be tax efficient in the process."

I GOT EXCITED when I saw how their assets were allocated—39 percent in Bucket One, 59 percent in Bucket Two, and two percent in Bucket Three. It was clear that we could execute the Bucket Strategy and have the potential for success. In his first three years of retirement, Brad had an effective tax rate of four percent in 2018, five percent in 2019, and four percent in 2020, with an income ranging from $106,000 to $166,000. "I expected to pay much higher taxes," Brad said. "To be honest, I have been a little surprised how low they have been, even though they told me it would. You don't know for sure until you experience it."

Today, Brad is in a very comfortable position and able to do what he wants. "I'm not worried about my income for the rest of my life," he said.

"Now that I'm retired, and the kids are getting married and having kids, I've helped them as much as I could, not having to borrow for a car, money to put aside for savings, and to purchase a house. My daughter just bought a new house in Illinois. She's moving, and she's 35, and they paid cash for it. That's something a lot of people can't do."

Brad is also able to commit more money to charitable giving. "I've always been very consistent with giving at least 10 percent to charity, and now I can usually give more. I started a charitable fund to send our friends when they go on mission trips and stuff … we can finance them. There are several charities that we give to regularly. We give to our church regularly."

As I've shown you, Bucket Two has the potential to help you with your major life expenses prior to retirement; it could also possibly allow you to retire much earlier than you thought if you are young and just starting. Even though you'll most likely pay more taxes on your Bucket Two investments during your accumulation years than you will on Buckets One and Three, you have the opportunity to make up for that during your distribution years when you qualify for a much lower income tax rate.

In the next chapter, I will show you the vital role Bucket Three plays in your retirement income and how those investments can be used to leave a substantial legacy of wealth to the future generations of your family.

CHAPTER FOUR

Positive Cash Flow, Tax-Free—Bucket Three

"If intelligence is our only edge, we must learn to use it better, to shape it, to understand its limitations and deficiencies-to use it as cats use stealth, as katydids use camouflage-to make it the tool of our survival."

- Carl Sagan

"The goal isn't more money. The goal is living life on your terms."

- Will Rogers

I f you are like most people, the percentage of your wealth in Bucket Three is usually the lowest. This is because, until 1997, the only financial vehicle you could use to accumulate wealth in this bucket was cash value life insurance. Let's face it … if you look up the question "Is cash value life a good investment?" online, you will probably find an equal amount of negative and positive opinions. But don't worry. Regardless of how you feel about cash value life, I will show you other strategies that I believe you can implement to fill your Bucket Three accounts.

First, let's have a history lesson to help you understand how Bucket Three investments came to be.

History of Bucket Three Investments

Senator William Roth was the principal author of the tax legislation that established the Roth IRA through the Taxpayer Relief Act of 1997. The Roth IRA gave taxpayers the option to invest money in a vehicle that allowed for tax-deferred growth and tax-free withdrawals, with fewer withdrawal restrictions than a traditional IRA and without all the internal expenses of cash value life insurance. Of course, with Uncle Sam involved, there was a catch. You were extremely limited on how much you could save each year, and if your income was above a certain amount, you were excluded from saving at all.

Year	Contribution Limit	Catch-up 50+ Year Old	Non-Working Spouse Contribution
1996	$2,000.00		$250.00
1997	$2,000.00		$250.00
1998	$2,000.00		$2,000.00
1999	$2,000.00		$2,000.00
2000	$2,000.00		$2,000.00
2001	$2,000.00		$2,000.00
2002	$3,000.00	$500.00	$3,000.00
2003	$3,000.00	$500.00	$3,000.00
2004	$3,000.00	$500.00	$3,000.00
2005	$4,000.00	$500.00	$4,000.00

2006	$4,000.00	$1,000.00	$4,000.00
2007	$4,000.00	$1,000.00	$4,000.00
2008	$5,000.00	$1,000.00	$5,000.00
2009	$5,000.00	$1,000.00	$5,000.00
2010	$5,000.00	$1,000.00	$5,000.00
2011	$5,000.00	$1,000.00	$5,000.00
2012	$5,000.00	$1,000.00	$5,000.00
2013	$5,500.00	$1,000.00	$5,500.00
2014	$5,500.00	$1,000.00	$5,500.00
2015	$5,500.00	$1,000.00	$5,500.00
2016	$5,500.00	$1,000.00	$5,500.00
2017	$5,500.00	$1,000.00	$5,500.00
2018	$5,500.00	$1,000.00	$5,500.00
2019	$6,000.00	$1,000.00	$6,000.00
2020	$6,000.00	$1,000.00	$6,000.00
2021	$6,000.00	$1,000.00	$6,000.00
2022	$6,000.00	$1,000.00	$6,000.00

With these low contribution and income limits, the Roth IRA got off to a slow start. Clients would ask, "Why open an account where I can only invest $2,000? It's just something else to look after, or another envelope to get in the mail." Or they would ask, "Will it even make that much difference in reaching my retirement goals?" I had to admit those were valid questions. Also, if I'm honest, financial professionals weren't all that motivated to recommend them because compensation was low. For example, if a financial professional worked on a commission basis and made three percent, they would earn $60; if they were fee-based and charged one percent, they would net a measly two bucks in a year.

Why the restrictions? Well, there's no doubt—tax officials in Washington worried that Roth IRAs were NOT in the government's best financial interest, long term. Leonard Burman, an economist and frequent financial publication contributor, once calculated that between 2014 and 2026, the U.S. Treasury could lose up to a total of $14 billion stemming from losses of conversions of (and contributions to) traditional retirement plans.

Roth IRAs picked up some momentum in 2001 when Congress passed the Economic Growth and Tax Relief Reconciliation Act (EGTRRA), which created a new form of retirement savings plan called the Roth 401(k). It was available as early as January 2006. However, companies were <u>very slow</u> to add this feature to their plans. For example, the largest companies in my backyard didn't add the Roth 401(k) feature to their plans until much later—J.B. Hunt in 2017, Walmart in 2020, and Tyson in 2021. Why? Primarily, it traces back to money: the administrative cost increases to keep, track, and separate pre-tax account values from Roth values.

A significant advantage of the Roth 401(k) over the Roth IRA is that the income and contribution limits are much higher. For example, in 2022, the Roth IRA contribution limit is $6,000 if you're under 50 and $7,000 if you're 50 or older (as opposed to the 401(k) limits of $20,500 and $27,000). If you're single and earn more than $140,000 or married-filing-jointly and earn more than

$208,000, you can't contribute to a Roth IRA. But you *can* contribute to a Roth 401(k).

Conversion Law Change

Roth IRAs gained more mainstream traction in 2010. Until then, you could not convert your IRA to a Roth if your adjusted gross income was more than $100,000, whether married or single. Not only was the $100,000 income limit law permanently repealed, but the government also allowed the taxes owed from conversions to be spread out over two years.

This was a huge win for my clients Sanjeeb and Jina, who are both doctors. We converted their $100,000 IRA to a Roth account. They spread out the $40,000 in income taxes over two years, and because of this, when they turn 60, they will have access to approximately $400,000 ... tax-free!

I hope you see why your Bucket Three wealth might make up the lowest percentage of your assets. It is due to a combination of low contribution and income limits, stifling tax laws, and companies not adding the Roth feature until very recently (even though they could have started in 2006). But the situation's improved dramatically since then.

Shut the Front Door

Our firm uses other strategies that help our clients bridge the gap much faster, but we have to go through the "backdoor" to get there. This is sneaky, yes ... but not illegal or immoral. Over 10 years ago, when I mentioned "backdoor strategies" to my clients, they were skeptical. Let's face it … any strategy that is called "backdoor" sounds sketchy.

The Backdoor Roth IRA is a way for people with higher incomes to sidestep Roth IRA income limits. Remember, in 2010, the conversion law changed to allow individuals making over $100,000 to convert traditional IRA to Roth. That is when this strategy was born. I would like to say I thought of it, but I don't need more reasons to ask forgiveness when I say my prayers tonight.

This approach boils down to some fancy administrative work. You make a <u>nondeductible</u> contribution to a traditional IRA and convert the funds to Roth the next day. The law says you have to pay taxes on any IRA money you convert that you deducted from your taxes, but *since you don't deduct it*, there are no taxes owed. Even though you didn't qualify to contribute to a Roth directly, you get to fund it through the backdoor anyway, regardless of your income. From there, your asset grows tax-free … and after age 59½, you can withdraw it tax-free. Uncle Sam is totally excluded from the conversation.

Mega Backdoor

This lesser-known strategy is available IF you work for a company with a 401(k) retirement plan that allows for <u>after-tax</u> contributions. If you are not sure if yours does, simply call your HR department (and if they don't, I would encourage them to add this feature). This allows for contributions up to $61,000 a year or, if you are over

50, $67,500 in tax year 2022. It's the same concept as the Backdoor IRA; since you didn't make "pre-tax" contributions, there are no taxes owed when you convert. Pretty awesome, right?

Cash Value Life Insurance

I'm fortunate to have started my career in the life insurance industry. Many professionals who start with investment companies have a negative bias toward cash value life insurance products. Not because of anything factual or objective, but because they don't understand them ... and therefore, they don't like them. I'm not quite as confined.

You don't have to "love" cash value life insurance. You don't even have to *like* it; you just have to like it a little more than you like paying taxes. If you want to simplify the debate on whether cash value life is good or bad, you only need to calculate if the internal expenses of a life policy are less than the 15 to 20 percent tax rate Uncle Sam charges you for capital gains and dividends in Bucket Two. And if you don't live in Wyoming, Washington, Texas, South Dakota, Nevada, Florida, Alaska, Tennessee, or New Hampshire, you get to pay state income taxes, too (California is the highest at 13.3 percent). When a policy is appropriately designed to maximize accumulation with a long enough time frame, I assure you—the internal expenses of cash value life are <u>much less</u> than Uncle Sam and your state tax.

Cash value life insurance also has some distinct advantages over its cousins in Bucket Three.

- No contribution ceiling.
- No income limitation.
- Access to your earnings without penalty before 59½.
- Potential death benefit to leave to heirs.

Accessing your money before 59½ is a big deal. Let's say you're like the Underwoods or the Marshalls, from Chapter Three. You want to retire early with an income greater than $109,250 and still enjoy a zero percent tax rate. If so, you can use cash value life insurance to supplement your income. (Yes, I know you can withdraw your Roth IRA principal without penalty or taxes, but you won't have very much principal to withdraw with those low contribution limits. For example, if you save $6K for 20 years, you'll end up with $120K. That will last maybe five years when you withdraw it ... *if* you are lucky.)

After our clients fully fund their Roth IRA, 401(k), and use all the backdoor strategies available to them, we recommend saving additional money in cash value life insurance if they also have a life insurance need and medically qualify for it. I won't go into detail here about the different kinds of cash value life insurance. But most of our clients have the proper risk tolerance and time horizon to implement variable universal life insurance because they want to assume the risk in exchange for controlling how their money is invested in subaccounts that are similar to mutual funds. Since this saving strategy is long-term, I counsel my clients to invest money in products that have the potential to perform better than fixed-rate investments, like bonds. Other cash value life insurance like universal and whole life policies pay a fixed rate each year determined by the insurance company and can be an option if you are a conservative investor.

Deferring Gratification—Pay Taxes Now So You Can Pay Less Later

I encourage most new clients to switch their pre-tax savings to after-tax Roth contributions. Usually, they cringe at the idea. It's only natural. Remember when we discussed Instant Gratification in Chapter Two? Most of my clients will tell you when they started following the Bucket Strategy, they didn't notice a significant impact when they invested pre-tax dollars vs. after-tax dollars. What <u>never</u> happened was that they saved less money, as the online calculators say should happen when you compare pre-tax and Roth. In the real world, people just <u>spend</u> a little less. Perhaps you cut out a coffee or two per week, or brown bag your lunch instead of eating out. But you won't have to give up vacations or other large ticket items. By choosing to defer gratification *now,* you may be able to save tens of thousands of dollars in taxes in your retirement years— dollars Uncle Sam ***can't collect.*** Imagine how much more comfortable you could be, the added legacy you could leave to your family, or the charities you could help, just by being a good steward of your wealth in your accumulation years.

The Switch: David Baskin

David is a vice president of merchandising in the meat department of Walmart. He was a saver, but like many of his fellow employees, he looked at it as an "either-or" part of life: either you save money, or you don't. He didn't think too deeply or strategically about how he saved. With a wife and the first of three children, David was diagnosed with cancer early in life. Walmart employees have excellent health coverage, but cancer doesn't only spike hospital bills, as the Baskin family discovered. According to the American Cancer Society, patients often face unpredictable costs like high co-insurance, deductibles, out-of-network care, treatment plans, medicine, and expenses traveling/staying/eating for treatment. "After going through all that, I wanted to make sure I took care of all my family's financial needs," said David.

When we began to work together, David suddenly realized his pre-tax plan would cost him money in the long term. Sure, he saved a little bit in payroll tax by funding his 401(k), but he was shocked when we projected his tax bill in retirement. After an in-depth look at the numbers, it turned out converting to the Bucket Strategy was both believable and doable for David. "Honestly, I didn't even notice the difference when I began to fund my new Roth 401(k) versus the old one," he added.

David Baskin's Projected Bucket Strategy with Planning

	Bucket One	Bucket Two	Bucket Three
Initial	54%	46%	0%
Projected w/o planning	60%	40%	0%
Projected with planning	42%	40%	17%

Ralph Panek—From Stressed to Blessed

Ralph Panek and I became friends when he moved into my neighborhood. We discovered that we were members of the same golf club. During some of our shared golf outings, finance and saving came up, and we grew our client/advisor relationship from there. Ralph had received limited financial advice throughout the years and tried mostly to figure it out by himself. He didn't think he needed to "put extra capital into getting the advice" that he now knows he needs. He had a friend in medical school who helped him navigate some of the basics and that was it.

"When I moved to Fayetteville and met Lance, my wife and I were straight out of medical training. She's a physician as well, and we were in the heavy debt phase," said Ralph. "We weren't accumulating much wealth at that point because of our medical school debts. We weren't earning the comfortable salaries we currently have. The year 2010 is about the time we began our accumulation phase, and that's about the time Lance came into the picture." Before that, Ralph and his wife, Katy, mostly felt the weight and stress of debt.

"When we started, Lance sat us down and looked at where our money currently was and laid out the Bucket Strategy in a very non-pushy way. He showed us the advantages of the Bucket Strategy." This is what they looked like:

Ralph Panek's Projected Bucket Strategy with Planning

	Bucket One	Bucket Two	Bucket Three
Initial	85%	20%	0%
Projected w/o planning	85%	15%	0%
Projected with planning	42%	22%	36%

"Starting out, I would say the majority of my money—what little there was at that point—was invested in a 401(k) that I had from a transitional job that I took between residency and fellowship," said Ralph. "I had an annuity ... some cash on hand ... those kinds of things.

"When Lance opened up the 'Pandora's Box' of the Bucket Strategy, that was a big revelation. I remember being awed by it because I didn't know you could do that. Nor did I think of the back-end tax implications of retirement. At that point, everything was so fresh. We had just had twins born at that time, moved to a new city, and I was naïve and uneducated about the financial world. I knew I needed somebody to give me some advice to transition from my 'DIY' perspective. The meeting with Lance came at a good time, and it's been a fruitful relationship since.

"One of the first discussions Lance and I had was about my 401(k) with the hospital, in which the hospital matched contributions," Ralph continued. "Luckily, there was an option to convert it to a 401(k) Roth. That was the strategy we chose—to take it out of Bucket One and put it in Bucket Three. That was when the 'lightbulb' moment happened. I remember being excited and coming back to some of my work partners and telling them, 'Hey guys, you need to think about this because what you don't think about is the tax implications on the retirement horizon.'"

Though it was early in the process and Ralph didn't have a large amount of money put into Bucket One, the tax-saving implications of moving from the traditional 401(k) to the Roth IRA were significant. He added, "Even if they take 50 percent of my 401(k) now to roll it over into the Roth, it's much better than the taxes I would pay on the $1 million or more that it would turn into in 30 years."

It's Never Too Late (or Too Early) to Take Back Control

Many older people, closer to retirement, feel like the Bucket Strategy has come too late to make a difference. Regardless of your age or remaining runway to build your wealth, this strategy can help you. The buckets you invest in and how you make use of the remaining years available may look different than if you'd started earlier, but it can still work to your advantage.

Similarly, many young people just starting in their adult lives and with new careers feel they can wait before investing in wealth-growing practices and spend their money enjoying themselves in the present. While this may be true, you have to ask yourself: Would I rather have a good time *right now*, or the ability to *retire and live comfortably* at a young age while paying the least amount of money to the government?

Alec Tahy—Motivated by Momentum

Alec Tahy learned the concept of saving at a young age. His father, a veteran corporate sales professional, invested in starting medical school trades. He made sure his children understood that wealth doesn't just "happen;" it is *earned*. He believed his children should learn the value of a dollar. He did this by teaching them that they had to pay half the price of their first car. If they saved a good amount of money (which Alec did), with their dad's help, they were able to buy a nice first car. If they didn't put much savings toward their first car (as Alec's brother did), they ended up with a clunker that cost more to maintain than purchase. Alec's dad also gave each of his children $10,000 to kick-start their savings and learn to invest and save. Alec graduated from college without debt thanks to his father's wisdom, guidance, and contribution to his future.

Learning about saving early on motivated Alec, and later, he and his wife, to grow their wealth and leave a legacy for their children. Before they moved to Arkansas, they mainly figured out investing on their own. They found one financial professional who was very traditional in his views, but he was not a good fit for their family and their goals. I met Alec and his wife personally, and after we became friends on the golf course, they became clients of our firm as well.

"Lance made it easy to create a financial map with the Asset Organizer," said Alec. "That was an 'aha' moment for me. It makes it personal, versus just seeing numbers others have done." Alec and his wife are in their late 20s, so their before and after percentages in Buckets One and Three in retirement have the most change because of the amount of time to accumulate for retirement.

Alec Tahy's Projected Bucket Strategy with Planning

	Bucket One	Bucket Two	Bucket Three
Initial	10%	85%	5%
Projected w/o planning	9%	91%	10%
Projected with planning	5%	43%	52%

Using the Bucket Strategy to grow their wealth gave the Tahys an early glimpse into the stability of their financial future. "You always think about how to pay fewer taxes," Alec states, "but paying less taxes in the present I realized would cause me to pay more taxes later. I would rather pay a little more now and reap the benefits of paying a lot less later."

Putting It All Together

Figuring out how and when to invest in each bucket is usually a topic of conversation with my clients. That's why we created the "Retirement Investment Flow Chart" that you can access at lancebelline.net to help answer those questions. Depending on how you answer, you'll get clarity to ensure you maximize in each bucket. By combining all three buckets, you can grow your wealth with balance. Then you can take advantage of how taxes work in retirement.

What Happens if Tax Laws Change?

This is probably the second most commonly asked question I get about the Bucket Strategy. One thing is for sure, in life and with our government: change. For example, the recent Build Back Better bill that did not pass put the Backdoor Roth IRA strategies I mentioned in chapter 4, that have been in existence since 2010, on the chopping block. Thanks Senator Joe Manchin! If you grow your wealth with balance in each bucket, I would argue that no matter the tax laws in 10, 20, or 30 years, you will be in the best position to take advantage of them. Diversifying how your investments are taxed in retirement is just as valuable as diversifying the asset classes you invest in. Right now, positioning your accumulated wealth so that when you make withdrawals at retirement you are treated like "the little guy" appears to be the most appropriate strategy. Our government's tax system, as currently constructed, is geared to protect them.

So, That's the Bucket Strategy. What Next?

Now that we've covered the Bucket Strategy and how it works, I want to show you some of the everyday habits that keep many of us from saving to our maximum potential. Do you want to make sure your children are millionaires? There's a strategy to potentially achieve that! As you'll see in the next chapter, it's not only *how much* you choose to save ... but also *when* you start saving.

CHAPTER FIVE

Roadblocks to Wealth Accumulation–The Human Element

——

"The investor's chief problem—and even his worst enemy—
is likely to be himself."

- Benjamin Graham

"Time is more valuable than money,
because time is irreplaceable."

- John Maxwell

Now that you have a better understanding of the Bucket Strategy and the importance of saving strategically, I want to discuss common misunderstandings and misconceptions about wealth accumulation. Over my 25+ years as a financial advisor, I've witnessed many clients' financial successes. I've soaked it up like a sponge, learning and taking notes on what they did to accumulate their wealth, what was most important and what had the most significant impact. I've studied their behavior regarding money and observed how they communicated about money with their family.

I've also watched many people make terrible mistakes with money. What they did (and, in some cases, did *not* do) that caused them to lose wealth, or not accumulate enough to retire, or pile up too much debt. Looking back, I have learned far more from people's mistakes.

I'm going to unpack those for you in this chapter.

My clients that accumulated a lot of wealth all have <u>one</u> thing in common: **They started saving for retirement when they were very young**. This allowed them to benefit from the two most impactful words in finance: "compound interest." Put simply, it's "earning interest upon interest." It's remarkable what happens when you combine time with compound interest. Albert Einstein once referred to it as the "eighth wonder of the world."

Mowing for Millions: The Dylan Radcliffe Story

Several years ago, while a senior in high school, my son's best friend, Dylan Radcliffe, asked if I would meet with him to discuss his finances. When Dylan was 16, his parents helped him to start his own lawn care business. As he made money mowing lawns, he invested in equipment, borrowed money (and paid it back) to further his business, and hired an employee. He takes the money he makes and pays his employee, invests some back into his business, and keeps some for himself.

My planning advice to Dylan was to fund a Roth IRA fully, invest in the S&P 500 Index, and never touch it, which he did. Starting at age 18, Dylan invested $6,000 every year in his Roth account. If he saves that amount every year for five years and *never saves another dime*, assuming a 10 percent return, Dylan will retire with over $1,200,000! Yes, you read that right … over **one million dollars, tax-free … from only investing $30,000**.

What if Dylan decided not to save for retirement until after college and saved the same $6,000 for five years? How much less do you think he would accumulate? It can't be that much, right? Well … only if you think $500,000 is "not much." At age 60, he would have $500,000 less, so waiting five years costs an arm and a leg—$100,000 a year.

Here's another example, with three investors, of how compound interest and time work.

- Britta starts investing $5,000 per year at age 18 and stops at age 28. She invested for 10 years for a total of $50,000.
- Braxton, at age 28, also invests $5,000 per year but doesn't stop until he reaches 58. So he invested for 30 years for a total of $150,000.
- Boden is the most diligent saver. He starts investing $5,000 at age 18 and doesn't stop until he reaches 58. He invested for 40 years—a total of $200,000.

Assuming a 7 percent annual return, their future values at age 58 are the following:

- Boden, $1,093,672
- Britta, $585,352
- Braxton, $508,321

Do you see the difference? Braxton invested three times as much as Britta and saved for 30 years versus her 10, yet has less money. Boden is the big winner here because he started saving early and never stopped.

The moral of these stories is that TIME is your biggest advocate (or adversary) for accumulating wealth. And the simple fact is <u>WHEN</u> you start investing typically outweighs how much you invest.

The Cost of Convenience

Sometimes young people tell me they wish they could invest but don't have the ability because all their money goes to bills. I can relate. I was young once, and I had terrible habits regarding *spending* money versus *saving* money. After I read Thomas Stanley's book, "The Millionaire Next Door," I changed my habits and started to save.

If you're like me, you don't think twice when you run into the store to pick up a cup of coffee or Coke on the way to work, or a quick fast-food meal at lunch, or order pizza on the way home because you don't feel like cooking. I would almost guarantee that if you tracked your spending faithfully and honestly on those things for a week, you would be surprised at how much money you spend on *convenience*.

We all do simple things every day that, under a savings microscope, would surprise us with the amount of money we waste. We are *all* guilty of it. Sometimes convenience, or "keeping up with the Joneses," is just second nature to us.

The $10,000 Coke

No, that's not a typo. Before you tell me I need to go back to second grade, let's think about this for a moment. Remember a few paragraphs ago, where I mentioned stopping by the store for a Coke every morning? When you look at it from a financial standpoint, that Coke will cost you **thousands** of dollars over your life. Let me explain:

Say you run by the store every morning or grab a Coke with lunch five days a week. We're going to average the cost at $1.50 per can. That's $7.50 a week ($30 a month). That doesn't seem like much, right? You pay more than that for a tank of gas. *However,* let's look at the long-term investment capabilities of $30 a month:

If you take $30 a month, invest it strategically for 14 years (before your kids ever leave high school) and make a 10 percent return on that investment, you would have $10,914! *Ten thousand dollars* in savings, just for giving up one Coke a day, five days a week.

But let's look at an even longer term ... say 48 years. I know that sounds like a long time, but would giving up a Coke a day, five days a week, for 48 years be worth

$425,223 to you? You read it right … almost half a million dollars! Now that's an expensive Coke!

Bring Back the Lunch Box

A young lady in my office named Morgan has two young children, and she's saving money so they can go to college. Instead of eating lunch out during the workweek, she brings her lunch to work, takes the money she would spend eating out, and invests it in the college fund. By taking the time to plan and bring her lunch, Morgan saves an average of $200 a month and invests it. In 18 years, with a 10 percent return on her investment, she will have over $120,000 saved for college expenses. When her children are entering their freshman year of college, do you think she's going to look back and wish she could've eaten out for lunch every day instead of taking the time to plan her meals? I don't.

When trying to find ways to save, look at the simple, everyday things you do. You will be amazed at how many of your hard-earned dollars you could find to invest in living comfortably in your retirement years (or to send your kids to college) just by giving up some of the little conveniences in your life.

Talking Finances—Why Saving and Investing Should Be Part of the Discussion With Your Kids

For many of us, money was a taboo subject when we were growing up. It wasn't discussed in front of the children, and especially not *with* the children. I'm not saying that our parents were wrong, but times have changed and aren't as simple as they used to be.

Most school curriculums do not have mandatory classes about how to manage money, so if our younger generation doesn't learn at home, they'll enter adulthood with no idea of what to do. They probably don't realize the budgeting that goes into electricity, groceries, transportation, or money for school. If money management is foreign to them, investing and saving for future needs and retirement will throw them for a loop.

Most parents think that their wealth (or lack of it) is "none of their children's business." After all, it doesn't become "the kids' money" until you pass away. In many ways, this is true, but opening up and having frank discussions with your children about money can set them up to be more successful and less dependent on you in their future lives. It can also allow you and your children to build generational wealth for years to come.

Holding money close to the chest until the day you die doesn't do your kids any favors. Especially as they mature into adulthood, and start raising your grandkids. Let me ask you: Who is in a better position to fund the grandkids' education—you, retired on a six-figure income with a three-figure tax burden ... or your 30-something daughter and son-in-law, as they fight to stay ahead of their mortgage payment?

Imagine that you put $30K in an education fund for your grandchild shortly after their birth. At a seven percent standard return rate, it would be worth at least

$105,000 by their 18th birthday. However, his mother and father—your adult child and their partner—would have to save $245 every month (or just shy of $60K altogether) to get the same amount ... *and they have to work for it!* You don't! You write one check in 60 seconds. It's the old tortoise-and-hare game, where "slow and steady" wins the race. As the grandparent, you part with $30,000. But you save your adult children <u>decades</u> of stress and pressure, not to mention $30,000 extra they would have had to save on their own!

If you play this game right, you can enable some of life's heaviest price tags to "skip a generation," the same way hereditary traits and personality quirks do. Remember the Knipples in Chapter Two? One of the things Richard and Cindy did was help their newly married daughter buy a house. What a difference it makes to be in your 20s or 30s and own your home, free and clear! What a position it would give *them* to begin bankrolling *their* kids' mortgages and grandkids' educations!

My friend, Steve Butler, works as a tax attorney, CPA, and estate planner. He understands how difficult it is to talk with children about finances, especially when they might be on different levels of awareness and understanding.

"As parents, we are not communicating with our children," Steve said. "We may love them all equally, but we have to plan for them differently. We have to empower them, to allow them to practice generosity.

"I'm not sure where I heard this, but it's out there everywhere," he added. "Approximately 70 percent of accumulated wealth doesn't survive the second generation, and approximately 90 percent doesn't survive the third."

So, how **do** you begin to teach your children about money? First, it's by realizing that understanding finances is more about *wisdom* than about age. Regardless of your children's ages, you can start teaching them simple lessons about saving money. If they get an allowance for doing chores, have them put part of it into savings so that they can watch it grow. As they get older, they will have the wisdom to keep doing this, and then you can teach them complex ways to make their money work for them (like Dylan). My colleagues and I start asking our clients to bring their children in when they are in high school to have what I call "Financial Planning 101." We teach them all about savings and investments, so they avoid the traps many college students fall into.

Brandon, the son of one of my clients, made a good point about talking to your children about money. "Every family is going to talk about finances. At some point, there's going to be conversations. It's either going to happen when the parents pass away, and the kids are sitting around the dining room table talking about how they're going to figure everything out, or it's going to be 'You don't have enough money for long term care, and we're trying to figure it out,' or it's going to be 'Wow! I didn't know mom and dad had so much money. What are we going to do with all this? I wish I would've known this 15 years ago because I wouldn't have done XYZ.'

"Every family is going to talk about money. It's *how* those conversations are structured and *when* you have them. I think that's the other part that's so important—the idea of 'Should I talk about it or not?' The conversation is going to happen. Are you going to let it control you, or are you going to control the narrative and the conversation and the topics?"

Family Investment Club

Another client, Doug Ramsey, and his wife found another way to teach children about finances.

"My father-in-law started a family investment club," says Doug, "for the entire family. Brothers, sisters, aunts, uncles, cousins, even the kids, too, to teach them how to save early.

"The family each agreed that they would put 'X' amount of dollars into an account each month—say, $100. Each family member would write 12 months' worth of checks (e.g. $100/month for 12 months = 12 checks) dated for each month. My father-in-law would then cash the checks each month, and the money would go into the fund. Every quarter the family would get together and discuss the portfolio—where it was going, what it was doing, what their investments were. They would then, *as a family*, decide to either shift, divest into something or invest into something and kind of present it to each other, but they had to have a majority rule to make changes in the investments. It was a good thing, a really good thing."

The family would also meet monthly with a larger investment group and a financial professional, which gave them the knowledge of the best areas to invest in. Doug's wife said that this allowed her parents to leave money to her and all of her siblings after they passed away and teach the family about investing.

"We went through some papers after my father-in-law passed away," Doug said, "and we found paperwork where he was able to help family members when they fell on financial hardships."

If you share financial wisdom with your children when they are young, you prepare them to be better stewards of their money as they age and start families of their own. As parents, we don't want to see our children struggling to meet the financial demands of adulthood. As Steve said, we must empower our children to not only be able to take care of themselves but also allow them to practice generosity—whether toward their children, family members in need, or charities. Our responsibility as parents is to arm our children with the financial knowledge they will need to teach future generations and stop the loss of generational wealth from the lack of that knowledge.

John & Karen–Teaching Generational Wealth

John worked at Walmart for 20 years in operations and then left to start his own company, which he's run for the past 18 years. I met John when he started his business in 2004. We did not begin using the Bucket Strategy until after John and his wife, Karen, became clients. However, we were able to help their children using the Bucket Strategy. "It will benefit the second generation (the kids) more than us, but we do get an advantage at this point from Bucket Two as small business owners," said John.

Unlike many parents of that era, John's parents talked with him about finances and investing. John and Karen openly discuss finances with their children.

"We always talked about saving and investing with our kids," Karen said. "It was a conversation we kept going, through all their years growing up. As they became adults, that conversation continued, maybe on a more advanced level. We've always taught the kids to work hard and know the value of a dollar, live below their means and be good stewards of their money, and hopefully along the way to have an entrepreneurial spirit."

Sharing financial conversations with their kids comes naturally to John and Karen. To them, it seems strange that more people don't do it.

"We had two empty lots, and we sold them to the two oldest children. Claire was just little at that time. They paid $26 a month, and they had to bring their check every month and get it signed off. We've always done things like that ... just kind of teach them along the way," said Karen.

Robert, John and Karen's son-in-law, married their daughter, Jennifer. He was surprised with how open they were when they started involving him in financial discussions.

"Jen and I started dating around the time John started talking about finances. I remember one of the very first interactions—he brought up the 'Rich Dad, Poor Dad' book series, and we were just 15 years old. I was just a stranger off the street, and he was already talking about investing and having your money work for you. I didn't know the family all that well. He's always been intentional about talking about finances, whether with his kids or someone else."

Jen knows that their parents' discussions with them growing up put them a step ahead of their peers.

"With them exposing us to things so early and having those discussions, we aren't afraid to make those decisions or step off the ledge a little quicker than some others our age would be. In the long run, that puts us that much further ahead because we made those investments starting in our early twenties, and we're not afraid to do it," she said.

John and Karen's son, Levi, agrees with his sister. "A key part of making my family and other families different when talking about finances is that it makes the family dynamic different when you are an independent business owner. When you're constantly pursuing new business plans and opportunities, that's what you talk about. It's not just your day job. It is your everything, every day. It's your livelihood. It consumes you more than a 50-hour-a-week job with a corporation would. I think that drove the conversation, him starting the business while we were young teenagers."

Levi went on to say, "I think we have benefited from business experience. I see in my friends that the first time they come to a big financial decision as an adult, it's the first time they've ever thought about it in their life. When they go to get a loan for their first home, they're relying on the banker to guide them through the process and help them pick, rather than having their own opinion, their own set of experiences, and prior knowledge on the processes.

"One thing that has benefited us is that as we've grown up, we have a base set of knowledge of what it is to be an adult, to invest our money, to save, to budget, to have a credit card, and bank account. I don't know about my friends, but I've had a bank account since I was 12 years old. It's things like that that set us up to have a head start on our friends. They have to learn everything anew when they're 26 years old. It's also an independence thing.

"I think the more you teach your kids about money and the more you put it on them, the more responsible they learn to be. Our parents pushed us to be independent money-wise and as people, rather than other people our age whose parents are holding the strings to everything they do until they're older, and then they barely let them go anyway. They're still controlling their children's financial life."

Can you see the "snowball effect" this starts, and how it alters the direction of your family tree? John's mother and father spoke openly about finances, and their transparency set he and Karen up to create a *culture* of generosity, fiscal discipline, and prudent investment. When we're open and inclusive of those we love in the financial decisions we make, it's amazing how they take <u>ownership</u> of the ideas and philosophy we want them to have. They're now creating momentum for generations that haven't even been *thought of,* let alone born.

John's life quote is, "You can give the kids the fish and feed them, or you can teach them to fish, and they can feed themselves." John believes, "That's the biggest part, teaching your kids to fish instead of them standing there with their hands out all of the time."

Small Business Owner or Corporate Executive?

Many of my clients are small business owners or corporate executives. The Bucket Strategy works for either one but may look different for each. In the next chapter, I will show you how to use it to your advantage for growing your wealth—no matter how you earn your keep.

CHAPTER SIX

Small Business & Corporate Executive Strategies

"The legal right of a taxpayer to decrease the amount of what otherwise would be his taxes, or altogether avoid them, by means which the laws permit, cannot be doubted."

- George Sutherland

Small Business Strategies

Small businesses get hit hard at tax time. Many people feel like the harder they work, the more they earn, but they bring home less money at the end of the day. Owning a small business is difficult enough without giving your hard-earned money to the government. Yet most small business owners hang their heads, sign the checks, and may even work twice as hard to pay twice as much the next time taxes come due. It can be discouraging and make people wonder why they stay in business for such little reward.

Most small business owners (or their accountants) are aware of standard deductions they can take on their taxes, such as home office, vehicles, startup costs, and ordinary costs of doing business. However, there are other ways to reduce your tax liability and keep more of your money.

The Most Important Decision You Will Make as a Small Business Owner

My business partner, Travis Riggs, works daily with small business owners. He says the owner's choice of how they set up their business from a legal and tax standpoint is one of the most important decisions they can make. How they do this will be a primary factor for lowering the amount of taxes they will pay during their working years.

A small business owner has to decide if they will be a sole proprietor, LLC, or corporation. The most common is an S-Corp. "In my opinion, that decision alone is the most tax-saving decision that clients are going to make, and it's made on day one," Travis said.

Why an S-Corp? "Because you can classify some of your income as <u>salary</u> and some as a <u>distribution</u>. "You are liable for self-employment taxes (Social Security and Medicare) on the salary, but not the distribution portion," Travis explained. "Let's say your total net income is $200,000 ($50,000 from salary and $150,000 from distributions). You're paying 15.3 percent in taxes on $50,000 instead of on $200,000."

Let's say you choose the option of a sole-member LLC in which all the profit is subject to self-employment tax.

This is how your income from the business would be taxed, assuming a 20 percent federal income tax rate:[5]

Income	Self-Employment Tax (Soc. Sec., Medicare)	Federal Tax (20%)	TOTAL TAXES
$200,000	15.3% ($24,028)	$40,000	**$64,028**

As you can see, that's nothing to write home about, especially when you factor in time. If you pay $64,028 in federal and self-employment taxes every year for 20 years, your lifetime tax bill is $1,280,560! So, let's look at the same chart, with the same gross income and federal tax rate:

Income	Self-Employment Tax	Federal Tax (20%)	TOTAL TAXES
Salary - $50,000	15.3% ($7,650)	$10,000	
Distributions - $150,000	-	$30,000	
Totals - $200,000	$7,650	$40,000	**$47,650**

Do you see the difference? Not only do you save $16,378 a year in taxes, but over the same 20 years, you pay $327,560 <u>less</u> to Uncle Sam! Wait ... it gets better! If you invested that annual tax savings into Buckets Two and Three assuming a 10 percent return, you would have over $900,000 accumulated at the end of those 20 years.

---

5   Social Security is only taxed up to the wage base (in 2022 that was $147,000). Formula: $147,000*.062=$9,114.00*2=$18,228+$5,800 (Medicare) (.029*$200,000)=$24,028

Travis continued, "Most new business owners are aware that they (as the employer) are required to withhold 6.2 percent for Social Security and 1.45 percent for Medicare tax from their employees' wages, and they have to match that. So the government gets 7.65 percent from the employee and another 7.65 percent from the employer. What owners usually miss is that in S-corps, they are simultaneously treated as an employee. So they are effectively paying 15.3 percent. The Social Security match is capped at $147,000 of income for 2022, but the Medicare tax of 2.9 percent is on ALL of your income. Even when you're saving the 2.9 percent Medicare tax after the Social Security match has been capped, if you've got a significant net profit, you're still saving a tremendous amount of money."

An important term the IRS uses to assess your salary is "reasonable." For example, if you make $500,000 and only designate $20,000 of that as salary income, you might trigger an IRS inquiry since you are avoiding so much self-employment tax. What constitutes "reasonable" can often be a grey area, so consult with your tax professional to be sure.

Another step you should consider taking if you're opening a small business is to see an accountant <u>first</u>. "Often, when someone thinks of opening a business, they go see an attorney first, and then an accountant. They have that in the wrong order," said Travis. "They should see a CPA first because we're going to give them more guidance and direction for how they need to structure their entity for tax purposes. For example, there is no such thing as being taxed as an LLC for federal income tax purposes. It is either taxed like a sole proprietorship, a partnership, or a corporation. We can talk through what their first year is going to look like and give them guidance for when they go to their attorney."

Learning & Earning Young: Paying Your Children to Work in Your Business

Even small children can work and do chores. As a small business owner, you should consider using that to your advantage while enabling your children to "earn and learn" by putting them on your payroll as W-2 employees. Your children will have to perform some type of service for your business. That service can be as simple as taking out the trash and cleaning, filing and organizing, or any other age-appropriate service they can perform. You only need to keep their W-2 income under the standard deduction for a single taxpayer (currently $12,950 in 2022), and you accomplish two things that are in your favor: 1. You lower your tax liability AND 2. You teach your children about money. Here's an example:

Your 10-year-old daughter, Julie, likes to help keep things clean. She can take out the trash, run a vacuum cleaner, and dust the furniture. Cleaning your office is a service, and therefore you can pay Julie to perform that service.

You pay Julie $249 per week to clean your office ($249 x 52 weeks = $12,950). Because you are paying Julie as a W-2 employee, you can take a tax deduction on every dollar for her pay. Better yet, because Julie's only source of income is equal to her standard deduction of $12,950, she does not have to file a tax return on that income because her taxable income is zero. This also gives Julie an earned income that she doesn't need (she's only 10), which can be used to fund a Roth IRA or a 529 for education, thus saving for her future. The money made can also be put toward the cost of extracurricular activities, such as vacations, sports-related fees, band fees, or other club fees or expenses.

By paying your child an income out of your small business, you're reducing your tax liability. They don't earn enough to pay income taxes, so they already have a retirement plan in place at a very young age and are learning how to manage, save, and invest their money. As long as you are careful and your children are old enough to perform the services they perform, this strategy is a potential win-win situation.

Making Business Pleasurable

We all love a well-deserved vacation. We scrimp and save all year long to have a week or two away from early mornings, late nights, and the stress of being a small business owner. What many business owners overlook, however, is that with some planning and the sacrifice of a few hours of vacation time, they can turn some of their vacation expenses into legal, deductible business expenses.

When you claim business expenses, the IRS looks at three things to determine if they are legally deductible;

- Was it ordinary?

- Was it necessary?
- Was it reasonable?

You can't fly from Florida to California, buy some office supplies, and write the trip off as a business expense because you can get those same office supplies in Florida. But you *can* fly from Florida to California for a family vacation, take some business cards and make some professional connections while you're in California (and document those connections). Maybe you could take one of those new connections out to lunch to discuss business and deduct part of those expenses on your taxes. You would be able to deduct your portions of the airfare, hotel charges, transportation to meet and greet the connections you seek out, and business lunch(es) you treated them to.

When deducting expenses in this way, be careful with the expenses you claim and *how* you claim them. You can't deduct the entire hotel expense because you have your family with you, just as you can't claim your whole family's airfare. Consult and confirm with your tax professional. Document your business-related movements and save your receipts, and then enjoy your now partially tax-deductible vacation.

Educate Yourself (and then deduct it from your taxes)

Did you know that the IRS will reward you for being a lifelong student? Every small business has an ever-changing learning curve. Whether it's new technology or software, learning relational skills to better communicate with your employees, or learning new business strategies to grow and scale, you must continuously educate yourself to stay in business. Tuition, supplies, and travel from your place of business to school are all potentially tax-deductible. Whether it's a privately taught course, a college course, a business seminar, or a session with a business coach, if it's related to your business, it can be claimed and deducted as a continuing education expense. (Consult with your tax professional. It is usually claimed under the section referred to as "Other Expenses.")

Remember that the IRS won't let you deduct for classes to move forward into a *different* type of business or career. To claim the educational expenses as business expenses, they must be related to the business you currently own.

Retire Confident & Wealthy

When you're a small business owner, you have complete control over what type of retirement plan you implement. You can design it to maximize your Bucket Three savings! Depending on whether you have employees, consider the following plans:

Small Business Owner with no Employees

An owner-only 401(k) with Roth features and profit sharing, that allows for maximum after-tax contributions. If you're married, both you and your spouse can participate. If it's possible, both of you should max out your Roth. If you need a deduction, then make a profit-sharing contribution. If you don't, then make an after-tax contribution (Mega Backdoor Roth) and then convert to Roth. This would allow both of you to save up to $61,000 a year (in 2022). That is $122,000 that you could save in Bucket Three!

Small Business Owner with Employees

Consider implementing the same 401(k) design as if you didn't have employees. Make sure it has the Roth features and profit sharing, and allows for after-tax contributions. Your choices include:

- Adopt a matching program that the government pre-approves (safe harbor).
- Customize a matching feature.
- Don't match at all.

Other plans exist for small business owners like Simple and SEP IRAs; however, you must be aware that these only allow you to contribute pre-tax to Bucket One. Consult with your financial and tax professionals to see if these options are more suitable for your situation.

Health Plans for Retirement

Small business owners have complete control over what type of health insurance plan they implement. You can design them to maximize an entirely new bucket category: **Bucket Four.** Health Savings Accounts (HSAs) are the only financial vehicle that allows you to deduct your contribution, grow them tax-deferred, and withdraw them tax-free (only when used for medical expenses)! Anyone can open and contribute to an HSA if their health insurance deductible and out-of-pocket costs are above the minimums below:

- The health insurance deductible for your family (in 2022) has to be at least $2,800 and $1,400 for an individual.
- Out-of-pocket expenses for your family (in 2022) must be at least $14,100 and $7,050 for an individual.

These are the most common questions/answers regarding HSAs:

- **How much can I contribute?** $7,300 for a family and $3,650 for an individual (in 2022).
- **Do I have to use the money each year?** No, I encourage my clients not to use the funds until retirement so they will grow and compound.
- **How is the money invested?** You decide low, medium, or high risk. Each HSA custodian has different investment options to choose from, just like an employer's 401(k) plans.
- **What happens at death? Where does the money go?** Your named beneficiary.

- **How do I access the money in the account?** You will be issued a debit card that you can use for qualified expenses and purchases.
- **What are qualified expenses?** Health care, dental, or vision expenses for yourself, your spouse, children, parents, and others under Section 152 of the tax code.

The following link is a great resource to find the right HSA for you:

https://20somethingfinance.com/best-hsa-account/

I've covered just a few of the ways to reduce self-employment tax liability and use the savings to fund and grow your retirement accounts. I highly recommend talking to your financial professional about other options to help you keep and save those hard-earned dollars.

Tips and Tricks for Corporate Executives

Bonus, Restricted Stock Units and Restricted Stock Options Strategies

If you're like many of our corporate clients, you dislike unexpected or unexplained costs. We found this causes our clients the most surprise and frustration because of … you guessed it … how these investments are taxed! So, before we discuss strategies to best utilize your bonus, restricted stock units, and/or restricted stock options, we need to review how your income is taxed.

Supplemental WHAT? Tom E's Story (New Walmart Exec Client)

"Why do I owe $35,000 in taxes?" Tom asked Travis after getting back his tax return. "I have the maximum withheld from my paycheck. I contributed a lot to charities; this is so frustrating!"

Travis then introduced two new words to Tom's vocabulary: SUPPLEMENTAL COMPENSATION. In short, this means income from bonuses, commissions, and other non-recurring types of payments or compensation. Basically, income other than your salary. The required federal income tax withholding is a flat 22 percent, up to $1,000,000 of income, and then it increases to 37 percent.

Walmart only withheld 22 percent from Tom's $150,000 bonus and his $200,000 restricted stock units (RSUs) that vested. Combining that income with his $300,000 salary, the 22 percent withholding is insufficient because his effective (<u>average</u>) federal tax rate is 32 percent.

"That's not true!" Tom replied. "Look at my pay stubs ... a lot more than 22 percent was withheld for taxes from my bonus and RSU payment! They withheld 35.74 percent!"

Travis said, "That is true, but not all of it went to pay federal income taxes." He then did the following math on a paper tablet:

22 percent is for federal income taxes
+6 percent is for state income taxes
+7.65 percent is for FICA

(6.2% for social security up to the maximum taxable wage base and 1.45% for Medicare)

+ <u>0.09 percent</u>

(additional Medicare tax since Tom's salary was greater than $250,000)

= 35.74 percent

So, in Tom's case, 10 percent of his $150,000 bonus is $15,000 and 10 percent of his $200,000 RSU is $20,000—hence his $35,000 tax liability.

The moral of this story is that the net amount of your bonus, RSU and/or options you receive is *not necessarily* all yours. Don't spend all of it because Uncle Sam may come knocking on your door at tax time.

When to Sell My Restricted Stock or Restricted Stock Options?

Deciding when to sell restricted stock or restricted stock options is very subjective, based on your situation, but here are some questions we ask and guidance we provide based on our clients' answers:

- How much vested stock do you have already? What percentage of your portfolio is your stock?
  - o It's very common for clients to get over-allocated in company stock because of the behavioral bias called "Familiarity." Human beings tend to prefer what is familiar or well-known. The guidance of a trusted advisor can help you to answer, "How much is too much?"

- Are you reluctant to sell it because of the tax liability?
  - o Guess what? There is no additional tax liability. You're already going to incur income taxes on the spread between the grant price and the fair market value of the grant at the time it vests. But if you sell as soon as they vest, there is very little to no additional tax because there is no capital gain incurred.
- What do your future grants look like? Are they larger, smaller, or the same?
  - o If your career is going "up and to the right," then the likelihood is that your future grants will get bigger. So it becomes harder to avoid getting overloaded with your company stock.

We use a software called StockOpter (stockopter.com) to help our clients decide how to maximize the value of their equity compensation. It is available for individual subscriptions as well. It provides clarity and insight on the following:

- Helps you decide when the optimal time is to exercise.
- Projects the equity compensation value lost when you leave your company before retirement.
- The stock price at which your financial goal is reached.

- The level of concentration in your company stock and options.
- The estimated tax effects of exercising options or RSUs when they vest.

To Defer or Not to Defer

Congratulations! Whether because of rank or income, you have qualified to participate in your company's deferred compensation plan. Do you participate, and if so, how much? To answer these questions, I need you to answer some other ones:

- Do they match your contribution?
- Is the return on your deferrals based on a fixed interest rate or a variable rate determined by investments you specified?
- What are the payout options? (e.g. only at retirement or at a specified age, lump sum or over 15 years)
- Does the plan give you a choice of payout elections each time you make a deferral?
- Why do you want to defer? To prevent excess spending or to accumulate wealth?
- Do you have a financial plan in place guided by trusted financial advisors?

Things to consider when contributing to a deferred compensation plan:

- If they don't match your contribution, don't participate.
- If it pays a fixed interest vs. allowing you to control how the money is invested, only participate equal to the company match.
- If the payout elections are very restrictive, be cautious. "One thing in life you can count on is change."
- Participating because your excess income will get spent (by you or your spouse) is <u>not</u> a good reason. As I illustrated in Chapter Two, you will pay more taxes to the government by deferring too much up front.
- As I have stressed before, it isn't about how much you save, but saving *strategically*—in proper amounts, in each bucket, with a distribution strategy planned in advance.

Maximizing Your 401(k)

Almost all companies offer 401(k) plans to employees who have worked at the company for six to 12 months. This is the most widely used financial vehicle to accumulate wealth for retirement. Here are the questions to consider when deciding to participate:

- Do they offer a Roth 401(k) in addition to a pre-tax 401(k)?
- Do they match your contribution?

- How many investment options do you have to choose from?
- Do they allow for "after-tax contributions"? If so, how much?
- Do they allow you to purchase company stock?

Things to consider when contributing to a 401k plan:

- If they offer Roth, then consider placing 100 percent in Roth up to the maximum allowed if your finances permit. If not, then only contribute pre-tax equal to the company match.
- If they don't have Roth (but they <u>do</u> match), then consider contributing up to what they match. If they <u>don't</u> match and <u>don't</u> have Roth, it might not make sense to participate if you take into account the future tax considerations.
- Having more investment options can allow you to customize your portfolio and better align with your risk tolerance and time horizon.
- If they allow for after-tax contributions, CONGRATS! You are eligible to take advantage of the "Mega Backdoor" strategy I shared in Chapter 4.[6] Contribute the maximum allowed, and then convert each year to Roth (if that option is available). If it isn't, convert it to a Roth IRA at retirement.

---

6   Contact your HR department to determine the maximum amount you can contribute based on their plan guidelines.

- Consider purchasing employer stock inside your 401(k) plan because it potentially allows you to save a bundle of taxes in retirement. The concept is called Net Unrealized Appreciation. It is too complicated to explain in detail here, but it allows you to pay capital gain tax rates on the gains instead of ordinary income tax rates. <u>Example</u>: $1,000,000 stock value, $50,000 cost basis, pay income taxes on the $50,000 and capital gain taxes on $950,000. Remember that zero percent tax rate in retirement? Exactly! Look up "Net Unrealized Appreciation" online to learn more, or contact your financial advisor for more information. If they are not aware of this strategy, I strongly encourage you to find someone who is.

Health Savings Accounts (HSA)

As I mentioned in the small business owner section earlier, this is the only financial vehicle that allows you to deduct your contribution, grow your funds tax-deferred, and withdraw tax-free (as long as it's used for medical expenses)! I'm a BIG FAN!

The most common misunderstanding for corporate clients is thinking they cannot contribute to an HSA unless their company offers one. The second most common misunderstanding is that they <u>must</u> use their company's HSA if they have one. *Neither of these is true!* Anyone not covered by a spouse's plan or by Medicare, with a qualifying high-deductible health plan, can open and contribute to an HSA if their health insurance plan meets the requirements below:

- The health insurance deductible for your family (in 2022) has to be at least $2,800 and $1,400 for an individual.
- The out-of-pocket expense limit in your high-deductible health plan for your family (in 2022) must be a maximum of $14,100 and $7,050 for an individual.

These are the most common questions/answers regarding HSAs:

- **How much can I contribute?** $7,300 for a family and $3,650 for an individual (in 2022), plus an additional $1,000 if you are age 55 or older.
- **Do I have to use the money each year?** No, I encourage my clients not to use the funds until retirement so they will grow and compound.
- **How is the money invested?** You decide low, medium, or high risk. Each HSA custodian has different investment options.
- **What happens at death? Where does the money go?** Your named beneficiary.
- **How do I access the money in the account?** You will be issued a debit card that you can use for qualified expenses and purchases.
- **What are qualified expenses?** Health care, dental, or vision expenses for yourself, your spouse, your

qualifying dependents and others under Section 152 of the tax code.

The following link is a great resource to find the right HSA for you: https://20somethingfinance.com/best-hsa-account/

So, we've covered how to save strategically (and the importance of it). We've reviewed roadblocks to avoid that will impact the amount of wealth you accumulate. We've looked at ways to utilize your benefit plans, whether for small business owners or corporate executives. It's now time to transition to charitable and estate planning strategies.

CHAPTER SEVEN

Estate Planning & Charitable Strategies

"By failing to prepare, you are preparing to fail."

- Benjamin Franklin

"Your greatness is not what you have, it's what you give."

- Anonymous

et's be honest: Nobody likes to do estate planning. It's one of the most common "unchecked boxes" when I talk to people about their financial planning. Not only can it be confusing, but also no one likes to think about death, even though we all know that the only two things guaranteed in life are death and taxes. James 4:13-14 in the Bible comes to mind: "Come now, you who say, 'Today or tomorrow we will go into this or that town and spend a year there and do business and make a profit.' You don't know about tomorrow. What is your life like? For you are a puff of smoke that appears for a short time and then vanishes."

In this chapter, you'll get a better understanding of your options for estate planning. If you've been blessed financially and don't know what to do with your assets when the curtain falls, read on. We've got several strategies and ideas for impact that go well beyond writing a check.

Estate Planning (The Basics)

Whether you know it or not, <u>you have an estate plan,</u> even if you don't have a will or a trust.

What Happens if I Die Without a Will?

If you die without a will, it's called "dying intestate." A local probate court takes over to decide how to distribute your property, by appointing a representative (or administrator). Most of the time this person is your surviving spouse, or one of your adult children. Until the court appoints a representative, your assets are frozen. They follow your state's intestacy laws to distribute your property. The order of succession usually prioritizes your surviving spouse, followed by your children, parents, siblings, and extended family members.

Who Takes Care of Your Children if You Die Without a Will?

Generally, the surviving parent gets custody of minor children if one parent dies. But sometimes, the surviving parent has passed away themselves or is incapable of caring for their children. In this case, the court will ask family members to volunteer as guardians. The court will give custody to whomever they decide will best protect your children's interests.

What is Probate?

Probate is the legal process administered by a judge in probate court to distribute your assets that don't have a beneficiary designation. The probate process can be slow and expensive, with guidelines varying from state to state. The larger your estate, the more complicated it tends to be.

Benefits of a Will

- You get to name your <u>executor</u> responsible for managing your estate and its proceeds through probate.
- You get to name <u>guardians</u> for your minor children. While minor children usually go to their surviving parents, you can name legal guardians to take care of your children if both of you pass away.
- You get to name <u>caretakers</u> for your pets.
- You can name <u>charitable organizations</u> you want all or part of your estate to go to.
- You can designate which of your <u>individual assets</u> go to certain people.

Benefits of a Revocable Trust

- <u>Avoids probate</u> and (most likely) distributes the estate to your heirs more quickly.
- May <u>save money</u> by avoiding probate, and they also <u>hold up better</u> than a will if someone comes forward to contest the distribution.
- <u>Protects your privacy</u>. It is a private document between the parties involved and does not become part of public record.
- Assists in the event of <u>incapacitation</u>. If you become ill or incapacitated, the person you choose as successor trustee can step in and manage your affairs without interference from a court.
- It gives you <u>more control</u> over what happens to your property after your passing.

Example: You can put language that your minor children don't get control of 100 percent of the money they inherit at age 18. You can spread it out to different percentages as they reach certain ages.

As a CFP® professional that guides and directs clients' comprehensive financial planning, I am usually their point man. When discussing estate planning, the most common question I get asked is, "Should I have a will or a trust?"

There's no simple answer. You can access a "comparison of estate planning options" guide at lancebelline.net to help clarify which option might be best for you.

Steve Butler, one of the best estate planners in Northwest Arkansas, had this to say: "The process varies from state to state. In Arkansas, I prefer to avoid probate. It can take as long as six months, there's no guarantee of privacy, and it can become expensive. By contrast, an Arkansas trust currently in force is acceptable, both at death and in the event of incapacity."

Steve pointed out some other important attributes of trusts:

1. A trust is the best way to plan for death AND incapacity.
2. Trusts help you avoid multiple probates. If you have property in multiple states, it's a no-brainer.
3. Trusts help you deal with your will for minor children. Unlike probate, there are far fewer barriers with trusts to pass your estate on to your kids effectively.
4. Trusts keep your estate plan private.
5. Trusts are much better for handling concerns with unhappy heirs or legal challenges to estate planning. You have a much better chance of working around those issues with a trust.

Deep Freeze, a Can of Beans & Sticky Notes

Communication with your loved ones about your estate prior to your death is essential. In a time of grief, the last thing you want them to have to think about is finding copies of wills, trusts, lists of assets, or who should get what from where and why.

"I always tell clients to find a 'safe spot' for their will or trust documents and make sure they tell the people who need to know where to find it," Steve said. "Sometimes I am surprised at where they choose their 'safe spot' to be.

"When one particular client died, the children called me and said, 'We can't find Mom's trust document. It's not in the safe. We found a note that said you had a copy.' I did have a copy, but we would need to have the court verify it to use it. So I asked them to keep looking. Over time the kids gave up, and as they got ready to sell the house, one of them called me to inform me they found the trust! This little lady had wrapped up her trust and put it in the *deep freeze* in her garage!"

Other clients put cash in even stranger places. "I had a client that buried money throughout the yard, and we had to dig it up," Steve said. "One recently told me she has tens of thousands of dollars hidden in a can of beans within her kitchen cabinet. 'Don't let them throw the can of dry beans away,' she said. 'There's a significant amount of cash in them.'"

Another of Steve's clients used sticky notes to designate who inherited each item from her estate.

"I had this family that I represented for some time. The husband had passed away. I represented the wife and then the kids. This lady was getting up in age, and we had worked hard to make sure her planning was exactly the way she wanted it to be. She had a tremendous amount of tangible personal property, from jewelry to a grand piano. We were talking about this, and she had some very strong feelings about where some of this should go, and it wasn't just to the children."

Steve explained, "There's not a form required for this.[7] It just has to be in the handwriting of the person, signed, dated, and described. But clients always ask for a form, so we developed a form. We give clients the form all the time, and tell them, 'You don't have to use this form, but if it makes it easy for you, go ahead.'

"My client asked if I needed a copy of this form. I told her I didn't, but to keep a copy of it with her estate planning and make sure that her executor (her oldest daughter) knew where to find it. The day after her funeral, the children, grandchildren, and I were at the house to go over her estate planning and the daughter gave me the estate planning files, and I was horrified when I flipped the pages, and there was the blank form that I had given her."

Steve told the kids, "Okay, here's the deal. Your mom and I talked about this for years. I know for a fact where she wanted some of the things to go, but this form is blank, so I'm not sure where to go from here. I hope we find it; this will be part of the treasure hunt.

"So we started talking about it and looking around ... 'Here's where mom's important papers are.' Nothing, nothing, nothing. Then a grandchild pulled a sticky note from inside of a lampshade, and grandma had written who she wanted to get that lamp, and she had initialed and dated it.

---

7   Most, but not all, states allow handwritten notes to direct property distribution. It was allowed in this individual's state of residence.

"One of the kids asked if that even qualified. I asked if any of the kids would object to it being done that way because, technically, it qualified. We get it, we know what she meant, she initialed it, dated it, signed it, and she's got somebody's name on it.

"That little old lady had taped everything in that house. We spent hours looking for Post-it Notes. A sad time became absolutely hilarious because that little old lady had taped everything, including the grand piano. I kid you not; I don't know how she did it. She was so feeble, she must have been doing it for years, but she had obviously ignored my form. It all worked out for the best. All of the tangible personal property got exactly to where she wanted it. Nobody fought about it. Everybody was actually kind of tickled that mom had done that."

Family Love Letter

The Family Love Letter is one of the best tools to help ensure good communication with your family (and probably one of the greatest gifts you can give them). This document lays out everything they will need to know upon your death, such as:

- Important information about you, such as Social Security and driver's license numbers.
- Where important records can be found.
- Names of important people such as your attorney, accountant, insurance agent, etc.
- Your financial and asset information.

- General information such as where to find keys or combinations, passwords, and e-mail addresses.
- Burial wishes/information.
- Family history.
- Special words you want to say or memories you want to recall for your family.

This letter won't replace a will or trust. But it's useful to help your family find the important documents and information they need, as well as a way for you to express your thoughts, desires, dreams, and hopes that you have for them. Visit https://www.familyloveletter.com/ to get guidance on how to write your letter.

Beneficiary Audit

Did you know the beneficiary you named for your IRAs and other employer-based retirement plans takes precedence over what you put in your will or trust? At death, whoever is the named beneficiary will inherit that account, even if it's an ex-spouse or your parents/siblings after you get married. I recommend doing a "beneficiary audit" every year with your investments and insurance policies, to ensure all your beneficiary information and legacy wishes are up to date.

My colleague, Kyle, has a client that would have benefited from doing a beneficiary audit. Her mother passed away, leaving her responsible for a sizable 401(k). Her mom always told her, "I'm leaving the money to you, and you can sort it out." The client had two brothers that she was to share the proceeds with, but the account and the tax liability that went with it were left solely to her. Neither her mother nor her brothers ever had a financial professional.

"Before I got involved, my client and her brothers had already had some discussions, and they came to the conclusion she needed to cash out and give them their thirds, which was over $100,000 each," Kyle said. "They didn't know that by doing this, it would have left my client with 100 percent of the tax liability on the 401(k) in addition to reducing her lifetime gift tax exclusion on anything given to her brothers over the $30,000 annual gifting limitation for her and her husband ($15,000 each)."

Kyle sat them all down and explained that their mother should have given each of them one third of the proceeds. But since she didn't do that, the most tax-efficient way to get the money to them was through an inherited IRA and stretch out the withdraws over 10 years. They initially didn't like the idea, but Kyle pointed out that if his client did the lump sum they all would get less and the government more because she would be liable to pay around 50 percent in taxes (federal-state), versus approximately 25 percent if they spread it out. As much as they wanted their money up front, none of them wanted the government to get so much in taxes, so they decided to roll the 401(k) into an inherited IRA.

Charitable Giving Strategies

We all have a charity or two where we give monthly support via automated bank draft. Or sometimes during the year, we might write a check. Here are three strategies that allow you to give large lump sums of money more tax-efficiently.

Gifting Highly Appreciated Stock

Many people don't think about gifting stocks to their charities of choice. Typically, they sell the stock and give the proceeds of the sale to the charity. By doing this, they lose 15 to 20 percent of the value of that stock to the taxes they have to pay on the proceeds of the sale. One way to avoid that is to transfer the stock to your chosen charity directly.

By gifting stock directly to a charity, you avoid having a tax liability on the sale of the stock, and the charity can then sell the stock tax-free, giving them more money than they'd receive if you sold the stock, paid the taxes, and donated the remaining balance. As usual, it's all about removing Uncle Sam from the conversation.

Donor-Advised Fund

One way to describe a donor-advised fund is like a "charitable investment account" with the sole purpose of giving to charitable organizations you care for. You can contribute cash, securities, or other assets and decide later which qualified charities you want to support. You get an upfront deduction for what you contribute, and there's no timeline to make withdrawals to give to charities. The money in the fund grows tax-free. Most funds have several investment options. They are some of the fastest-growing charitable giving vehicles in the United States because they are easy to set up. Once you make your contribution to the fund, it is irreversible and cannot be returned. So make sure you are comfortable with the amount you put in. A simple online search will expose you to numerous financial institutions that have them.

Family Foundation

When thinking about how to be generous to the charities you wish to support, you should put some thought into creating a family foundation for charitable giving. Creating a family foundation is not difficult, but you must follow all IRS set-up and annual administration guidelines. You can appoint your children to the foundation's board. You then meet once a year during holidays, family vacations, or a planned date to decide the amounts of the gifts for the year and which charities will receive them.

Aside from the benefits to the charities, your family foundation enables:

- Opportunities to make decisions as a family.
- Involvement of younger children in decision-making, and teaching them to be generous, thoughtful, and charitable.
- Ideas for charitable giving that you might have overlooked.
- Learning about which causes matter to your family members.

A family foundation for charitable giving also gives you some tax advantages, meaning the government gets less of your wealth. These tax advantages include:

- Immediate tax deductions upon a donor's initial gift.
- Reduction in estate tax liability due to charitable gifts.
- Investment earnings, capital gains, and some other types of income aren't subject to income tax.

You've worked hard throughout your life to be a good steward of your wealth and to be able to leave a lasting legacy to your family. Giving them the gift of planning will provide them with the opportunity to celebrate your life without the stress of trying to figure out what you wanted, or where essential documents may be.[8]

Now that we've got the *unpleasant* parts of having wealth out of the way, let's move forward and look at how to continue to grow your wealth throughout your retirement years and have a little fun!

---

8   The strategies and ideas mentioned in this chapter are for informational use. Always consult with your own tax and legal professionals regarding your specific estate planning needs.

CHAPTER EIGHT

Retirement Income of the Future

—

"In order to grow we must be open to new ideas ... new ways of doing things ... new ways of thinking."

- George Raveling

"The only way you can sustain a permanent change is to create a new way of thinking, acting, and being."

- Jennifer Hudson

Congratulations, you made it! Your financial plan indicates you've accumulated enough wealth to retire and start withdrawing from your investments in each bucket, tax efficiently. If you're like my clients, you ask yourself the following questions:

- What happens if the stock market crashes?
- Will I run out of money?
- What investment strategies can I use to protect my retirement income?

Several different asset classes can make up your retirement portfolio. I'm not going to get into the weeds of how you mix all these investment types. I want to narrow our focus on the two main investment types—stocks and bonds. I will put forth several compelling reasons as to why you should consider dividend stocks as an important part of your retirement portfolio.

Your investments need to produce <u>income</u> and grow in retirement. The <u>income</u> component is very important. This means that whether your investments are growing or not, they produce <u>income</u> for you and your family. (Do you notice the emphasis on "income"?)

Dividend Stocks vs. Bonds

Generally, the older you get, the higher the percentage of safer investments (like bonds) you should own. They are less volatile and provide fixed income payments—things retirees need and prefer. In case you don't know how a bond works, the following graph will show you.

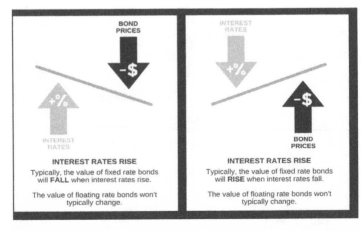

INTEREST RATES RISE	INTEREST RATES RISE
Typically, the value of fixed rate bonds will **FALL** when interest rates rise.	Typically, the value of fixed rate bonds will **RISE** when interest rates fall.
The value of floating rate bonds won't typically change.	The value of floating rate bonds won't typically change.

Retirees like bonds because they're straightforward and more predictable than stocks. But here's the rub: stable, steady income (the same dollar amount every month) doesn't account for INFLATION—the silent killer of value. During periods of inflation, every passing day "picks away" at your assets. The following shows the value of $50,000 affected by inflation.

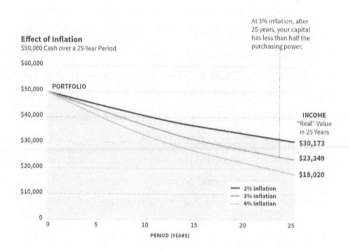

At three percent inflation, after 25 years, your $50,000 will have less than <u>half</u> of its original purchasing power.

The current interest rate environment, which is at historical lows, does not favor a strong allocation of bonds in a retirement portfolio. The following graph shows how, if interest rates go up, the value of bonds goes down. Likewise, if interest rates fall, bond values go up.

Look at the following chart of the 10-year Treasury bond, which is the benchmark used to decide mortgage rates across the U.S. It's also the most liquid and widely traded bond in the world. You don't need a degree in economics to know that the most likely direction interest rates have to go is up. Not only can you <u>not</u> get a bond paying four percent anymore, but, considering the average rate of inflation, there is a good chance your one to two percent bond will decrease in value between now and when it matures.

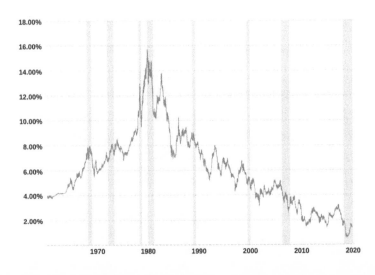

Asymmetric vs. Symmetric Risk

Michael Lieberman of Advisors Capital Management explains it best: "Bonds expose you to <u>asymmetric risk</u>. You get the same return, whether the company's booming or not. With stocks, you have *symmetric* risk. You participate in the upside when the company does well; you participate in the downside when it goes poorly. Bonds are different. You will never participate in the upside ... but, if the company fails, you have the potential for the entire downside. Lehman Brothers' collapse in 2007 is a good example: if you owned one of their bonds paying four percent, your annual upside was four percent, give or take underlying bond price fluctuations. In 2008 your downside was effectively ... 100 percent."

Although cases like these are rare, you need to ask: Is the downside worth it? Just look at the Great Recession's biggest bankruptcies: Lehman Brothers, Washington Mutual, General Motors, Chrysler, General Growth Properties, Colonial Bank, and Bank United. As a bondholder, you have preferred status for collection during bankruptcy and you may not lose 100 percent like the stockholder. This is true, but collecting pennies on the dollar is a minimally positive result.

Dividend Aristocrat to the Rescue

So how can you secure a predictable income that grows over time and helps withstand inflation in retirement? Consider dividend-paying stocks.

Did you know some companies have not only *paid* a dividend each year but have *increased* dividends every year for the last 25 consecutive years?! Not only do you get the income you need in retirement, but you also get the growth that these companies returned over that time. Does this chart look more appealing to you?

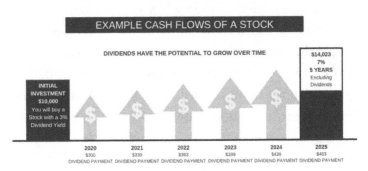

The S&P 500 Dividend Aristocrats index comprises 65 stocks that pay and increase dividends every year. To be in the index, companies must:

- Be members of the S&P 500.
- Be valued at least $3 billion.
- Perform at least $5 million in quarterly transactions.

The minimum number of stocks needed to make up the index is 40. A company's inclusion on this list does not guarantee that it will always increase dividends, but it is worthy of consideration.

Dividends 101

A dividend is a small portion of a company's earnings. They're paid based on how many shares you own. If a company pays $1 per share and you own 100 shares, you will receive $100. A common misunderstanding is that the dividend will increase if the stock price increases, and vice versa. So the $10,000 you invest that buys you 100 shares in ABC company can go up and down in value. But the $100 dividend will continue to get paid to you as long as the board elects to continue to pay the $1 per share.

Larger companies are the most likely to pay dividends. Start-ups and high-growth companies like tech firms rarely pay them because their profits are reinvested to help sustain growth and expansion. Dividends are not guaranteed, and they can be increased, decreased, or eliminated at the board's discretion.

22-Year Case Study

I wore #22 for the Lamar Tigers, where I attended school in Missouri, and I wanted to give them a little shout-out.

To understand why dividend stocks should make up a significant percentage of your retirement portfolio, I enlisted the help of my good friend and colleague Michael Lieberman (mentioned earlier). We researched and documented stock prices and dividend history dating back to January 1, 2000, through August 31, 2021. We examined four stocks that should sound familiar to you: Home Depot (HD), McDonald's (MCD), Johnson & Johnson (J&J),

and Walmart (WMT). We compared them to a bond paying four percent, with a $20,000 initial investment.

	Initial Investment	Total Interest/ Dividends	Future Value	Total	Gain
Bond	$ 20,000.00	$ 17,600.00	$ 20,000.00	$ 37,600.00	$ 17,600.00
HD	$ 20,000.00	$ 23,014.68	$ 81,000.54	$ 104,015.22	$ 84,015.22
MCD	$ 20,000.00	$ 47,698.73	$ 217,215.89	$ 264,914.62	$ 244,914.62
J&J	$ 20,000.00	$ 39,554.09	$ 140,905.03	$ 180,459.12	$ 160,459.12
WMT	$ 20,000.00	$ 15,386.20	$ 80,627.88	$ 96,014.08	$ 76,014.08

Every one of these (except Walmart) paid more income than the bond. McDonald's and Johnson & Johnson more than doubled the bond income. And how can you ignore a minimum 4X return? In case you wondered, all these stocks are in the Dividend Aristocrat Index!

Let's make this real for you. Let's say that back in 2000, you purchased a Toyota Camry you planned to keep for 22 years. According to AutoTrader.com, the MSRP in 2000 was $26,198. After buying the vehicle, you invested $20,000 in the bond and these four stocks so you could have enough money to purchase a new Camry 22 years later.

2021 Toyota Camry MSRP: $35,620
- **Bond (total of $37,600)** – One Toyota Camry (Your wife will LOVE it, but only if you can afford to pay the sales tax.)

- **Walmart (total of $96,014.08)** – Two Toyota Camrys (Now you're BOTH rolling in style, plus you have cash left over!)
- **Home Depot (total of $104,015.22)** – Three Toyota Camrys (How about that Sweet 16? Your daughter/son will worship the ground you walk on!)
- **Johnson & Johnson (total of $180,459.12)** – Five Toyota Camrys (Now you've got the family fleet rolling!)
- **McDonald's (total of $264,914.62)** – Seven Toyota Camrys (Not only do you have the family fleet, but now you can impress your parents-in-law and buy them one, too!)

With numbers like these, you might say to yourself, "Investing in dividend stocks is a no-brainer." On the face of it, I agree—but nothing is ever as simple as it appears. To win at this game, you would have had to endure many years of *losing* money. These stocks did not go up consistently, year in and year out.

- With Johnson & Johnson, you would have lost money six of those 22 years (or 27 percent of the time). Their most significant one-year decline of 11 percent was in 2005, and two years in a row (2007-08) they lost 14 percent. (Does anyone remember the "talcum powder" lawsuits?)
- Walmart also had six losing years. The most significant loss came in 2015, when the share price

decreased 22 percent (thanks, Amazon). From 2002-05, the stock declined three out of the four years.

- McDonald's, the biggest winner, also caused the most stress. They had eight losing years, or 36 percent of the time, including two stretches of two-year declines from 2000-02 and 2012-14 (primarily from the national healthy food bandwagon and the NYC soda purge). Their most significant one-year decline was in 2002, where they lost 48 percent! (For a fun fact ... guess what year was its best? The very next one—2003. That year, their price went up by 81 percent.)

- Home Depot also faced six "down" years. The worst ones were 2002 and 2007-08. Remember the housing crisis? During both of these slumps, the stock price declined by 58 percent. (But how do you like them now, in the aftermath of 2020 and the lumber shortage?)

Here's how this looks:

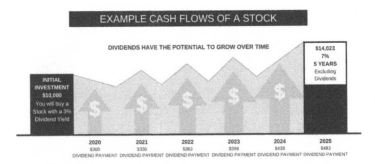

One thing these companies did, boom or bust, year in and year out, was pay <u>dividends</u>. And they not only paid them ... they *increased* them. If you owned these stocks, your retirement income grew <u>every year</u>, as long as you held onto your shares. And guess what also grew every year? INFLATION. In order to have the same spending power 10 to 20 years into retirement, you need an investment strategy that increases its income and keeps pace with that dirty little "I" word!

Just the Facts: Education About the Market and Investing

Even with these staggering numbers, the likelihood you'll invest 100 percent of your money in dividend-paying stocks is low—because of the volatility that goes with it. *But what if you did?!* The additional wealth you could create would be incredible. To help you think through this, I want to share the following market facts to help you understand what's "normal" with the stock market—so that when crazy things happen, you are less likely to overreact and lose perspective. No one likes surprises in life. But with investing, you have to adhere to the famous quote: "Expect the unexpected."

Intra-Year Declines vs. Calendar Year Returns

From 1980 through August of 2021, the S&P 500 Index has averaged 14 percent returns. But did you know that the index has been negative <u>every</u> year, at some point? We have <u>never</u> experienced positive returns, all year long.

That's not to say it couldn't happen, but why let yourself get all worked up in a frenzy when the market goes down? Historically, this has been the case dating back over 40 years. In fact, on average, the S&P 500 Index loses five percent or more about three times a year, lasting around 40 days each. A 10 percent decline, on average, occurs about every 16 months and lasts about 132 days. So train yourself to shrug when this happens. EXPECT IT.

Bulls vs. Bears

Sorry to throw in some financial language here, but to explain in simple terms, "bull markets" are when the market is up 20 percent <u>from previous lows</u>, while "bear markets" are when the market is down 20 percent <u>from previous highs</u>. Do you want to know why you make money in the stock market over the long term? It's because, since 1942, the average bull market period lasts 4.4 years—with an average cumulative total return of 154.8 percent. Meanwhile, the average bear market period lasts an average of <u>11.3 months</u>, with a cumulative loss of -32.1 percent. So bull markets historically last longer and go higher when compared with how long bear markets last and how much they lose. It has been shown that bull markets tend to climb slowly over time while bear markets occur abruptly and with little warning.

Normal Volatility

Almost every year, a client will say, "Lance, this market is going crazy, isn't it? It's having such big swings! What do you think is causing it?" They don't understand that the market, on average, from 2009 to August 2021, has one percent increases or decreases 63 days each year. So, out of the approximately 253 days a year that the stock market is open, for at least 25 percent of the time, the S&P 500 is going to have more than a one percent swing in a day.

The Market is Rarely Average

If you look back at the calendar year returns of the S&P 500 from 1961 to 2020, one thing should stand out: how RANDOM the returns are. Most of the time, they're up. Sometimes they're down. But in those 60 years, the market has only performed within two percent of its long-term average—six years. Practically, that means we're only "stable" for about 10 percent of the time! For the other 90 percent, we have to manage our emotions, curb our excitement with the big winning years, and not get freaked out when the market loses.

A major allocation of dividend-paying stocks can position your portfolio to have the potential of growth long after you have retired. Not only can they provide income during your retirement, but they can also provide the potential for you to leave a significant amount of wealth to your family as part of your lasting legacy.

This is my life's work—to show you how to grow your wealth strategically, while stewarding it well. The Bucket Strategy is a systematic way to potentially increase your wealth while being very tax efficient. It has worked for many of my clients, and it may work for you.

In the final chapter, we'll cover the value of having a financial professional and outfit you with tools to continue the journey.

CHAPTER NINE

A Financial Advisor's Real Value

———

*"The fact that people are fallible is your biggest
enduring advantage in the accumulation of greater wealth.
The fact that you are just as fallible is the biggest
impediment to that very same goal."*

- Daniel Crosby

To Behave or Not to Behave

n the fall of 2010, I drove to South Dakota with my colleagues for our annual pheasant hunt. I had purchased Nick Murray's audiobook, *Behavioral Investment Counseling*, for us to listen to during the 14-hour drive. The team didn't think too highly of my plans until we started listening. Not only did we listen to it all the way to South Dakota, but we also listened to it all the way back. It changed my life as a financial advisor forever.

Before that, I was like most of my peers in the industry. I thought I could add value by developing a unique investment strategy for clients to give them higher returns with less risk or a proven methodology for getting in and out of the market at the right time. Today, I know better. *Managing clients' behavior* is what leads to superior long-term returns. In the modern world, investing has become a commodity. Technology has improved so much that it's easy to find automated portfolios to invest in … just search online for "Robo advisor." If you go to a financial professional for their investment strategies, or if they tell you that they have a unique investment strategy, you and they are missing what really moves the needle. I know this doesn't sound sexy, but it's true.

Statistics support this. Dalbar Inc., an independent investment research firm, studied investor performance data since 1984. They publish an annual report that shows how it trails S&P 500 index returns, usually by 1.5 to two percent. Russell Investment Group did a similar study from 1984-2019 with the Russell 3000 Index and found that investors trail the index return by just over two percent. Why? In short, <u>fear</u> and <u>greed</u>. It's scary when the stock market goes down and people stop investing and start selling. When markets go up, they go on buying sprees. This flies in the face of the first rule of investing: "Buy Low, Sell High."

Behavioral science explains that we are <u>wired to make bad choices</u> with investing. We have limited abilities to process and respond to information. During bad times, we are prone to become irrational. My role as a financial professional is to help my clients recognize when it happens, like a counselor. The following are some examples of behavioral biases.

Overconfidence. We think we know more than we do, and we're more skilled at something than we are. When investing, this usually leads people to overestimate their understanding of financial markets. They invest in higher risks and ill-advised attempts to "time" the market—when to get in and out. To help my clients with this, I introduce perspectives and possibilities the culture and media ignore.

Availability. People use the most <u>accessible</u> information to make decisions, even when it might be incorrect. For example, people choose to invest in a mutual fund or stock because they recognize the brand, while overlooking or ignoring that it doesn't fit their strategy or help them reach their goals

Anchoring. Rather than consider all the facts, we hitch our wagon to ONE fact we like. For example, people look at the 52-week high-low price of a stock. If it's closer to the 52-week low, they think, "That's a good buy." In fact, the stock could still be overvalued, but those details don't matter if you're trying to find facts that you like.

Hindsight. We believe we know what the outcome will be beforehand—like the "Monday morning quarterback." If you buy a stock and the price falls, you think, "I knew it was going to fall," and become pessimistic about investing. Similarly, if it goes up, you think, "I knew that was going to happen," and you become overconfident.

Confirmation. We seek out information that aligns with what we already believe, and ignore information that contradicts it. With investing, if you have a favorable opinion of a particular stock and read articles with positive and negative reviews, you will give greater weight to the positive articles to validate your purchase.

Loss Aversion. We may be more motivated by *fear* than aspirations. The pain of losing money is twice as bad as the pleasure of making it. So when the market goes down, we become more erratic and eager to sell.

When things go wrong in life, or you feel impacted negatively, you feel like you should "do something, even if it's wrong." If you have a headache, you take Ibuprofen. If your car makes funny noises, you take it to a mechanic. If you're in physical pain, you see a doctor. Whatever it may be, you try to *fix* it.

With investing, when we lose money because the market goes down, we naturally think we should do "something." But with investing, doing <u>nothing</u> is often the best decision. Historical data shows that when the market goes down, it WILL come back if you give it enough time. Kyle Schiffler, a member of my advisor study group from Minneapolis, makes a great point: "The market bats 1,000 percent. Who or what else in life has that track record?"

If you study your own weaknesses and resist the urge to let them control your behavior, you can retire wealthy (and early). Moreover, you can grow a generational legacy that will benefit your family long after you have passed through the Pearly Gates.

Roofing Your House

Kyle had more wisdom to share about client emotions that he experienced during the Covid-19 pandemic.

"I have a client who's been with me for almost 20 years," he said. "She came to me when her mother died. She was the sole beneficiary of her mom's sizable 401(k) plan.

"It was right before the pandemic in March of 2020. We set a meeting with her and her brother. At the time, the market was in freefall, and the account's value had decreased by 10 percent. The first thing they said to me was, 'We have to sell mom's account. We're losing so much money. Get us out immediately; we've got to go to cash.'

"It was one of the most difficult calls I ever had. I was dealing with my client's emotions and with her two brothers—who I didn't know, and who didn't know me. My client had complete confidence in me, but her brothers had never worked with a financial advisor, and the more they talked, the more emotional they got. They were positive that selling was the right thing to do. I was positive that it was not."

In the time that it took Kyle's client to get the 401(k) rollover completed into her beneficiary IRA, the market fell another 15 percent. "Now, I had not only my client," Kyle said, "but also her husband and brothers demanding that I cash it out—again! We arranged another meeting to have further discussion.

"I told them, 'Just because the market's going crazy right now doesn't mean we should panic with your mom's 30 years of life savings. We don't panic during these times. We do what's prudent. And what's prudent is to stay invested.'

"It happened to be pouring down rain that day, so I asked them the question: 'When do you repair your roof?'

"They asked, 'What are you talking about?'

"I said, 'If your house needed to be re-roofed, would you do it today?'

"No," they responded, "that would be stupid. It's pouring down rain!"

"Well, that's what you're telling me to do with your mother's account," I said. "Currently, the market is pouring. It's thundering ... and you want me to re-roof the account—go to cash." That analogy clicked with them, and they agreed to wait out the rainstorm.

Kyle and his client reinvested the money on March 20, 2020. The market low was March 23. At the time of this writing two years later, the account is up 69 percent and the family now thinks Kyle is a king. "Without me to manage their emotions, there is no doubt that they would have sold the stock at one of the worst times of the market," he told me. "The money would've been put into cash and not reinvested."

The Foolish Act of Market Timing

It is only natural for you to want to participate in good markets and sidestep bad ones. But listen to me very closely ... YOU CAN'T. The S&P 500 is too unpredictable for you to "duck in and out" with precision. Data shows that missing only a small number of the market's best days has resulted in extreme underperformance. As recently as within the last decade, missing the top 50 highest-performing days could take you from earning 11.55 percent down to -5.58 percent.

When you exit the market, it feels like you're acting rationally. It doesn't make sense to invest when the market goes down, and you lose money. But if you do it that way, you have to make the right call ... twice! You have to get out at the right time (the high), and you also have to get back in at the right time (the low).

Thoughts to Control Your Emotions With Investing

When the going gets tough on the investor roller coaster, I hope these give you some peace of mind and confidence to stay the course:

- Never let short-term volatility impact your long-term financial plan.
- When the market goes down, remind yourself that <u>no one</u> in the media or any "expert" can predict its bottom. It's *all* speculation to get you to watch, subscribe, or click.
- Every bear market brings out people who say, "This time it is different" because bear markets are unexpected and often unexplained.
- Look at any long-term stock market performance chart. The line goes up and to the right, with dips, pullbacks, corrections, and bear markets along the way. It's a one-sided mountain that keeps growing over time.
- "Volatility" is different from "loss." *Volatility* is normal; it's what the market does. *Loss* is something that happens when we sell.
- Over the long term, you make most of your money in bear markets. You're simply unaware while it happens.
- A good financial professional doesn't try to insulate you from short-term losses. Doing so would jeopardize your long-term gain.

Finding the Best Financial Advisor for Your Family

I would imagine, if I were in your shoes and wanted to engage a financial planner, I would ask myself two questions: "Where do I begin?" and "What questions do I ask?" Most likely, you will address the first question by asking your peers who they use. I agree—that would be a great start. You can also go to cfp.net and click on "Find a CFP® Professional" on the home page. Enter your town and zip code, and away you go.

I enlisted my study group partners, and we compiled a "Top 20" list of questions you should consider asking when interviewing a financial advisor. As financial professionals, we know the questions that need to be asked, but often go unanswered. I hope you find it helpful. It's available at lancebelline.net.

The value of a financial advisor doesn't *always* lie in their knowledge of finance. Sometimes, we're behavioral counselors, relationship counselors, and more—if we're genuinely committed to the client. It's about people's lives and how money affects them, one way or the other.

Luis Strohmeier—More Than Just a Financial Advisor

"I have clients that have been married over 50 years; they've been my clients for 30 years," said Luis. "They were friends of mine before that, and I used to coach their son in tennis.

"About eight years ago, Ron (the husband) was at the height of his career, and I remember him calling me and saying, 'Things are going terrible at home, and I think I want to get a divorce.' My response was, 'Ron, how does Lynn feel about this?' Ron responded, 'She's sick of it, too. We both want to talk to you and figure out how we're going to go about this.'

"I called Lynn separately, and she stated she was sick of him. She said, 'He's selfish, and I can't stand him.' They were set in stone, and they wanted a divorce. I talked to the three adult children, who are also clients, and they agreed it was over. They were resigned that their parents' marriage was over."

Luis went to meet with his clients, sat them down, and said, "I'm just going to paint a picture of what it's going to be like if you divorce. I'm not saying that you need to stay married, because this is a matter of personal choice. I will say to think long and hard before making this decision because it's irreversible once you make it. Once you put yourself on this path, it's going to be very difficult to go back.

"I took all their assets. They've been married all of their lives; there wasn't one separate asset. I just divided everything in two. When it came to the house—a gorgeous house that was their dream house, that they'd been living in for almost 30 years—I put in there, 'Scratch the house. Neither one of you can have it. Neither one of you can afford it on your own. It's too big. You can't maintain it, so, boom! Out of the house, and now you have to buy two houses.'

"I started going through, and both of them were silent. They both said, 'Hold on, hold on.' Then Ron said, 'It doesn't seem like we should be getting divorced.' Lynn said, 'This is worse than I ever thought. If I'm going to be miserable, I might as well take the less miserable life.'

"Once they were done with the conversation, Ron and Lynn decided not to get divorced. I said, 'You're saying you don't want to get divorced because it's not financially feasible. I wanted to go through this exercise so you are committed to staying married, but it's not going to happen automatically. You made a financial commitment to be married. You made that commitment today. Now I want you to make the emotional commitment to stay married, fall in love with each other again, and find common ground on your differences. I'm not the one to help you, and you both need help, so you need to go see a marriage counselor.'"

Ron and Lynn told Luis they didn't know a counselor, and didn't want to ask their friends because they didn't want them to know. Luis knew one he could recommend.

"About a year and a half into seeing the therapist, Ron and Lynn rekindled their marriage," Luis continued. "Today, they have a beautiful marriage. They're retired, happy, and they've found new hobbies that they can do together.

"I think that it's not so much the financial aspect of it, but I'm proud I was able to help a couple stay married and have a happy life. Sometimes people get divorced for the right reasons, but sometimes they get divorced for the wrong ones. I think it takes us as financial professionals to identify that. If we start with the financial aspect, it gets their attention, instead of getting involved in the emotional side and getting kicked out of the house."

A Life and a Living: Lindsey Pruitt

For many financial advisors, Lindsey wouldn't have been the most interesting prospect. Being young, she didn't have the kind of wealth that translates into hefty fees. But my colleague Dax took her on because we've always believed that *anyone* who wants to learn and follow guidance is worthy of our time and effort. And Lindsey was as diligent as they come. She did <u>everything</u> Dax showed her how to do. She was fortunate to earn good money early in her career and diligently save and invest instead of spending it. That discipline allowed her to transition out of corporate life at a young age. If all her savings were in Buckets One or Three, she wouldn't be able to do what she does now.

As her portfolio grew, Lindsey's priorities shifted. In 2015, following a tragic personal event, she became a Christian and found herself looking differently at her corporate career. She felt called toward the mission field and wanted to participate. But she wasn't sure if doing it would torpedo everything she'd worked to build for herself financially. She was also looking to make good on Dave Ramsey's advice, and pay off the mortgage on her home. She'd enjoyed a tremendous year at her job, where she earned some massive commissions. She approached Dax to ask his advice. After a two-hour conversation, Lindsey was convinced that the money would perform better in her portfolio than in her home.

You may believe (as I do) in being 100 percent debt-free. Maybe you think Lindsey should have paid off her house. She is on track to do that, but we didn't want her to "step over dollars to pick up pennies." If she'd put that extra money into her house, it's true—she would have paid off the mortgage. She could earn 100 percent of the rental income instead of the amount she keeps today after expenses. But remember: *if you say "yes" to one thing, you say "no" to something else.* Lindsey's investments compound, year after year, as they grow in Bucket Two. When she retires, she'll have an awful lot more to live on and give away than a few hundred extra dollars in rental income. She earns four percent in dividends, while she pays 2.8 percent mortgage interest. Even if the stock market doesn't grow, she is ahead by 1.2 percent.

That decision turned out to be pivotal. With Dax's help, Lindsey could see a path to quitting her corporate job and devoting herself to full-time missionary work. She now lives abroad and pays her way through a combination of rental income and savings. "I still fundraise 100 percent of my costs," she said, "because I feel as though God wants me to involve other people who might not have any other way they can participate in the mission. But this decision was not scary at all after we did the math." On the day I connected with Lindsey to hear her story, I asked her, "What did you do *today*?"

She said, "Well, I went out for coffee with a friend, and we met someone and shared the Gospel with him. Now this evening, we're going out to dinner as a group, and we'll see what happens ... you never know who's going to pop up that we can tell about Jesus!"

Younger Me: What I Would Have Done Differently

I love the song "Dear Younger Me" by MercyMe. As the title suggests, it's about writing a note to your younger self. It starts, "If I could tell you everything that I have learned so far, then you could be one step ahead" and goes on to say, "Even though I love this crazy life, sometimes I wish it was a smoother ride." Sometimes this song makes me stop and think back to when I started as an investor-professional. This is what I would say to my younger self:

- Don't think for one minute that you can predict the future of the market. That is not rational. You can only depend on it in the long run.
- Don't think you can develop a unique investment strategy that gets better returns than the market.
- Don't get caught up in the media hype during bad markets. They are there to sell advertisements and need viewers/readers.
- Open and max fund your Roth IRA at age 18, and never stop.
- Engage with a trusted financial advisor that you can partner with in life. Preferably a CFP®.

Finishing Well

What I've learned to do, since we can't turn back the clock, is dwell on my <u>future</u> self—to make promises to start doing what I can with the time I have left.

Throughout this journey, I've tried to guide you on ways to be more tax-efficient with the money you work hard to earn. I've endeavored to enable you to leave a lasting legacy through generational wealth and the generosity of gifting to charities. Now, it's up to you to take the steps necessary to make that dream a reality.

Pull out a piece of paper, and tell your future self what you're going to start doing differently today to change your family's financial future.

- Have you completed the Asset Organizer to forecast your future wealth in each bucket? (Visit www.lancebelline.net for resources.)

- Do you need to make any changes to how you save money?

- Do you have clarity of what to invest in? Use the Investment Flow Chart to give you direction. (Visit www.lancebelline.net for resources.)

- What spending habits do you need to adjust to increase your savings? Use the expense planning worksheet to give you guidance. (Visit www.lancebelline.net for resources)

- Want to get a better understanding of the tax brackets, standard deductions, contributions limits to retirement plans, etc.... check out the tax facts at a glance guide. (Visit www.lancebelline.net for resources).

- If you're self-employed, do you need to change the type of retirement plan you have or how you are compensated to lower the amount of taxes you pay? Do you have children that need to be put on the payroll?

- For corporate executive readers, remember to set aside additional money for taxes from your bonuses and stock grants. Use the Investment Flow Chart to maximize your company benefit plans. If you're eligible, fund a Health Savings Account.

- Do you need to get your estate planning in order? Still a little unsure whether a will or trust is better for you? Check out the will vs. trust comparison. (Visit www.lancebelline.net for resources.)

- Complete a family love letter?

- Conduct a beneficiary audit for your investment accounts and insurance policies?

- Sit down with your family to talk about where you are financially and where you want to be.

- Create a family investment club.

- Create a family charitable fund, foundation, or invest in a donor-advised fund.

- If you're a grandparent with more than you can spend, open up a Roth IRA for your grandchildren and/or invest a lump sum in their education fund to maximize the benefits of how money compounds.

- Commit to finding the right financial professional that fits your needs. (Visit www.lancebelline.net for resources.)
- Review your investments. Do you need to change how they are allocated?

In Closing

I wrote this book to help people grow their wealth, go from "good to great" financially, and plan and implement strategies to pay the lowest amount of taxes. I've been surrounded and exposed to some bright and talented financial professionals over the years, and soaked up their wisdom like a sponge. I wanted to share everything that I learned, to show you a path that may change your life. If I can help just one person, this has all been worth it. If just *one* family takes this advice and changes the next generation's ability to grow their wealth, it's worth it.

If you have questions or would like to talk further, get in touch at lancebelline.net. All are welcome; I don't care if you have $10 or $10,000,000. If you have a financial concern or question, I am here to help.

I firmly believe divine intervention caused me to become a financial planner. I want to use the gifts God gave me to give people peace of mind, clarity and tax efficiency over their financial goals. I hope you become a better steward of your finances because of it.

God Bless,
Lance Belline

GLOSSARY OF FINANCIAL TERMS

401(k) – A retirement savings plan offered by many U.S. employers with tax advantages to the saver. Employees can have a percentage of each paycheck deposited directly into the 401(k) account, and the employer can exercise the option to match the contribution.

Accumulation Phase – The "working years" of a person's life, usually between ages 18 and 65, prior to the retirement-oriented "distribution phase."

Backdoor Roth IRA – A retirement savings account for individuals with high incomes to sidestep the income limits of standard Roth IRAs. The investor makes a nondeductible contribution to a traditional IRA and immediately converts it into a Roth IRA. They pay taxes on the conversion, but the remainder of the funds grow tax-free in perpetuity.

Bond – A fixed-income investment where an investor lends money to a company or government for a set period of time, in exchange for regular interest payments. Once it reaches maturity, the bond issuer returns the investor's money.

Capital Gains – The IRS' tax category for income you earn from the sale of assets, such as real estate or stocks, or passively through the growth of ownership in a company, such as dividends.

Cash Value Life Insurance – A form of permanent life insurance that features a cash value savings component. Contributions and profits can be used for a number of expenses, such as self-lending or paying premiums. It is also the only tax-free retirement savings product with no income or contribution limits and accessibility prior to age 59 ½.

Certified Financial Planner™ (CFP®) – A designation awarded to financial professionals certified through the rigorous education, training and ethical standards of the CFP® Board

Certified Public Accountant (CPA) – A license given to accounting professionals who meet the Board of Accountancy standards in the state where they do business.

Deferred Compensation – A portion of an employee's pay set aside to be paid (and taxed) at a later date. Retirement, pension and stock option plans are examples.

Distribution Phase – The later years of a person's life, usually after age 65, where they either cannot or no longer need to work full-time.

Economic Growth and Tax Relief Reconciliation Act (EGTRRA) – Legislation passed by Congress and signed into law by President George W. Bush. It lowered income tax rates, placed new limits on the estate tax and allowed for higher contributions to IRAs and new categories of employer-sponsored plans, such as the Roth 401(k) and Sidecar IRA.

ERISA – The Employee Retirement Income Security Act of 1974, passed by Congress and signed into law by President Richard Nixon. This act created new minimum standards employers and fiduciaries must follow to ensure retirement plan assets are not misused.

Exchange-Traded Funds (ETFs) – An investment product that tracks a certain sector, index, commodity or other asset, but that can be traded or sold on a stock exchange the same way a regular stock can.

Individual Retirement Account (IRA) – A savings account with tax advantages individuals can use to save and invest long-term. Available through a bank, investment company, broker or online brokerage.

Internal Revenue Service (IRS) – The United States government's tax collection administration, a component of the Department of the Treasury.

Mutual fund – An investment program funded by shareholders that trades in diversified holdings and is professionally managed.

Ordinary Income – Wages earned through salary, bonuses, tips and other compensation in exchange for labor or services provided; and (secondarily) income from pre-tax investment sources, such as 401(k) or traditional pension retirement accounts.

Roth 401(k) – An after-tax savings account offered by employers, where employees can save and invest funds and withdraw them tax-free after age 59 ½. Taxes are deducted immediately when the employee is paid, but no further taxes apply on contributions or profits earned throughout the lifetime of the fund.

Roth IRA – A savings account where individuals can save and invest after-tax dollars and withdraw them without incurring taxes after age 59½. Available through a bank, investment company, broker or online brokerage.

Rule of 72 – A formula used to estimate the number of years it takes to double the value of an investment at a given annual rate of return. Assuming a $10,000 investment and an annual rate of return of four percent:

Divide 72 by the annual rate of return (4 in this case – but do not divide using .04)

72 divided by 4 = 18

Therefore, it will take approximately 18 years for your investment to value at $20,000

Stock – A portion of ownership in a for-profit enterprise, such as a corporation

Taxpayer Relief Act of 1997 – Legislation passed by Congress and signed by President Bill Clinton to reduce capital gains tax rates. It also created an entirely new class of tax-free retirement savings options, which led to the popularity of Roth IRAs and other tax-free alternatives to traditional retirement savings plans.

Traditional IRA – A savings account with pre-tax advantages individuals can use to save and invest long-term. Available through a bank, investment company, broker or online brokerage.

W-2 – The IRS code category for standard wages earned from labor or providing service to an employer. The opposite of "1099," which designates self-employment.

DISCLOSURE

This book is not intended as legal or tax advice. Accordingly, any tax information provided herein is not intended or written to be used, and cannot be used, by any taxpayer for the purpose of avoiding penalties that may be imposed on the taxpayer. The tax information was written to support the promotion or marketing of the transaction(s) or matter(s) addressed and you should seek advice based on your particular circumstances from an independent tax advisor.

The information in this book is not investment or securities advice and does not constitute an offer or solicitation of any kind. The commentary in this book is informational only and reflects opinions, viewpoints, and analyses of Lance Belline, which are subject to change any time without notice. Nothing herein constitutes a recommendation that any particular investment, product, transaction, or strategy is suitable for any specific person. Any mention of a particular investment or product is not a recommendation to buy or sell that investment or product, nor is any mention of a particular strategy a recommendation to utilize that strategy. There are investment techniques and strategies that may be suitable to an individual, but may not be discussed in this book. Individuals should speak with a financial professional before making any investment decisions. All investing involves risk, include entire loss of principal invested.

The quoted testimonials have been voluntarily offered by the provider cited who is a current or former investment advisory client of Lance Belline. The names of some clients have been changed to protect the identity of the client at the client's request. These statements reflect individual opinions and experiences and do not indicate or suggest broad suitability of any investment/financial advice or the advisability or potential performance of any investment, investment strategy or financial product or service, nor should they be relied upon as bases for any financial decision. Equitable Advisors, LLC and its affiliates do not guarantee the accuracy or applicability of the information included in any client statements or testimonials.

Links are provided for convenience to websites produced by other providers or industry-related material. Accessing websites through links directs you away from this book. Neither Lance Belline nor Equitable Advisors, LLC is responsible for errors or omissions in the material on third-party websites and does not necessary approve or endorse the information provided. Users who gain access to third party websites may be subject to the copyright and other restrictions on use imposed by those providers and assume responsibility and risk from use of those websites.

An index is a hypothetical portfolio of securities representing a particular market or a segment of it used as an indicator of the change in the securities market. Indexes are unmanaged, do not incur fees and expenses and cannot be invested in directly.

Equitable Advisors, LLC (member FINRA, SIPC) (Equitable Financial Advisors in MI and TN) is a registered broker-dealer. Securities products are only offered to clients or prospective clients where Equitable Advisors, LLC registered representatives are properly registered.

Equitable Advisors, LLC is a Registered Investment Adviser. Advisory services are only offered to clients or prospective clients where Equitable Advisors, LLC investment advisory representatives are properly registered. No advice may be rendered by Equitable Advisors, LLC unless a client service agreement is in place.

Travis Riggs, CPA (AR Insurance Lic. #3820592), is a participant in the Equitable Advisors Trusted Advisors® program as a registered representative of Equitable Advisors, LLC (member FINRA, SIPC) (Equitable Financial Advisors in MI & TN), an investment advisory representative of Equitable Advisors, LLC, an SEC-registered investment advisor, and as an agent of Equitable Network, LLC (Equitable Network Insurance Agency of California, LLC). In this capacity, Travis participates in a split of the commissions and fees generated in specific products purchased through Lighthouse Financial's engagement with their clients.

Lance Belline and duly registered/licensed associates of Lighthouse Financial offer securities through Equitable Advisors, LLC (NY, NY 212-314-4600), member FINRA/ SIPC (Equitable Financial Advisors in MI & TN), offer investment advisory products and services through Equitable Advisors, LLC, an SEC registered investment advisor, and offer annuity and insurance products through Equitable Network, LLC (Equitable Network Insurance Agency of California, LLC; Equitable Network Insurance Agency of Utah, LLC; Equitable Network of Puerto Rico, Inc.) Individuals may transact business, which includes offering products and services and/or responding to inquiries, only in state(s) in which they are properly registered and/or licensed. Lighthouse Financial is not a registered investment advisor and is not owned or operated by Equitable s or Equitable Network.

Equitable Advisors, Equitable Network, and their Financial Professionals, Agents and employees do not provide tax or accounting advice or services. You should consult with your own tax professional regarding your particular circumstances. Travis Riggs' CPA practice is entirely separate from his role with Equitable Advisors and Equitable Network, and Travis Riggs, CPA, is not owned, operated, or in any way affiliated with Equitable Advisors or Equitable Network.

References to individual tax liabilities are for illustrative purposes only. Each individual result and tax ramifications will vary.

Items for consideration when funding a Roth 401(k) account:

When an individual switches from funding a pre-tax 401k account to a Roth 401k account on an after-tax basis and maintains the same funding level, the individual will most likely be exposing more income to taxation if everything else remains the same. This will potentially create an increased tax liability due to an increased recognition of income for that particular tax year. The individual, under some circumstances, may have to make adjustments in spending elsewhere to account for the upfront payment of income taxes on the Roth contributions.

For comparison purposes, if the same amount is being invested in the 401(k) (before-tax funding) and the Roth 401(k) (after-tax funding), it assumes the tax on the Roth 401(k) is being paid from other income. A comparison of projected after-tax retirement income should take into account the taxes paid on the Roth 401(k) contributions.

Roth 401(k) plans are subject to Required Minimum Distributions beginning at age 72. The plan may be rolled to a Roth IRA to avoid RMDs, but withdrawals may not be available until after five years.

Employer matches to Roth 401(k) contributions can only be made to the traditional 401(k). These contributions and the growth on the contributions are taxed when withdrawn.

How a Qualified Charitable Distribution Works:

Normally, a distribution from a traditional IRA incurs taxes since the account holder didn't pay taxes on the money when they put it into the IRA. But account holders aged 70½ or older who make a contribution directly from a traditional IRA to a qualified charity can donate up to

$100,000 without it being considered a taxable distribution. The deduction effectively lowers the donor's adjusted gross income (AGI).

To avoid paying taxes on the donation, the donor must follow the IRS rules for qualified charitable distributions (QCDs)—aka, charitable IRA rollovers. Most churches, nonprofit charities, educational organizations, nonprofit hospitals, and medical research organizations are qualified 501(c)3 organizations. The charity will also not pay taxes on the donation.

For more information about Equitable Advisors, LLC you may visit https://equitable.com/crs to review the firm's Relationship Summary for Retail Investors and General Conflicts of Interest Disclosure.

CFP® and CERTIFIED FINANCIAL PLANNER™ are certification marks owned by the Certified Financial Planner Board of Standards, Inc. These marks are awarded to individuals who successfully complete the CFP Board's initial and ongoing certification requirements.

PPG-4505279.1 (3/22)(Exp. 3/24)

ABOUT THE AUTHOR

ance Belline, CFP®, CHFC®, is a 25+ year professional in the financial services industry. He founded Lighthouse Financial with one employee in 2005; today, Lighthouse Financial consists of 8 employees, 10 advisors, and 2 CPAs with over 1 billion in assets under management and clients in over 40 states.

He considers it his life's work to give people financial peace of mind and clarity regarding how they reach their financial goals. Lance knows that his clients' largest expense in life will be the cost of taxes. Therefore, he focuses on implementing financial plans that reduce that tax liability over their lifetime, allowing them to leave a larger legacy.

Lance lives in Fayetteville, Arkansas, with his wife Jessica and three children. His life is centered on his faith, being the best husband and father he can be, and making the most of the days he has been given.

A free ebook edition is available with the purchase of this book.

To claim your free ebook edition:

1. Visit MorganJamesBOGO.com
2. Sign your name CLEARLY in the space
3. Complete the form and submit a photo of the entire copyright page
4. You or your friend can download the ebook to your preferred device

Print & Digital Together Forever.

Snap a photo

Free ebook

Read anywhere

CPSIA information can be obtained
at www.ICGtesting.com
Printed in the USA
JSHW021705201022
31928JS00003B/4